53, The Singing Yacht.

Max Liberson

© 2015 Max Liberson.

All rights reserved by Max Liberson. The text of this publication, or any part thereof, may not be reproduced or transmitted in any form or by any means, electronic or mechanical, including photocopying, recording, storage in an information retrieval system, or otherwise without prior permission of the author.

While the author has taken all reasonable care in the preparation of this book the author makes no representation, express or implied, with regard to the accuracy of the information contained in this book and cannot accept any legal responsibility for any errors or omissions from the book or the consequences thereof.

All trademarks acknowledged.

ISBN: 978-1-326-43668-1

Dedicated to my good friend Edmund Whelan.

Table of Contents

Acknowledgements. 9

Chapter 1. 11

Chapter 2 15

Chapter 3 19

Chapter 4 21

Chapter 5 25

Chapter 6 29

Chapter 7 33

Chapter 8 37

Chapter 9 41

Chapter 10 43

Chapter 11 47

Chapter 12 51

Chapter 13 55

Chapter 14 59

Chapter 15 61

Chapter 16 65

Chapter 17 69

Chapter 18 73

Chapter 19 79

Chapter 20 83

Chapter 21 87

Chapter 22	93
Chapter 23	95
Chapter 24	99
Chapter 25	103
Chapter 26.	107
Chapter 27.	117
Chapter 28	123
Chapter 29	129
Chapter 30	133
Chapter 31	137
Chapter 32	141
Chapter 33	147
Chapter 34	153
Chapter 35	159
Chapter 36	165
Chapter 37	169
Chapter 38	179
Chapter 39	185
Chapter 40	191
Chapter 41	193
Chapter 42	197
Chapter 43	201
Chapter 44	209
Chapter 45	213

Chapter 46 217

Chapter 47 221

Chapter 48 233

Chapter 49 243

Chapter 50 249

Chapter 51 255

Chapter 52 259

Chapter 53 263

Acknowledgements.

One of the great things about being able to write this book is to say thank you to all the people who have helped me, from my crews Dave Norman, Mick Newman, Dave (pigtailed) Schooling, Helen Wood, and Wido Verlinde. I would also like to thank Paul Wells for instructing myself and Wido in the black arts of Carbon fibre sandwich construction and how to use epoxy resin, and various other facets of boat construction. It was extremely illuminating and very enjoyable. Dick Durham Kath and Mike Peyton deserve my heartfelt thanks for their encouragement and I hope they find this book entertaining.

My good friend Martin Bailey has once again agreed to format this work and send it off to the publisher. I also have to give a special thank you to Eva O'Donovan for being my fiancé and allowing me to go off sailing for half a year when I needed to!

Front cover picture courtesy of Sunsail UK.

Chapter 1.

The long Atlantic voyage was over, Gloria my Ferro schooner I had bought for £1500 slept peacefully at the end of the river Crouch, leaning on the wall my cousin owns by the antiques centre at Battlesbridge. Her bow was only a couple of feet away from the bridge that marked the very end of navigational opportunities, (unless you were in a kayak). The big building that loomed over her was the old Granary that the Thames barges used to load from. Before road transport and traffic jams with choking exhaust fumes became fashionable people used to have their grain moved about by these efficient sailing machines, along with other farm produce such as hay. In a really neat bit of economics, the barges used to take the hay up to London and come back with Horse Dung for the fields. But the barges are gone now, apart from "the British Empire" rotting gracefully a little further down the river. A reminder of how things were before "progress" increased the population and we really started to wreck the environment.

I was broke, as usual, and I needed work. Asking around brought various small maintenance jobs on friend's yachts. The problem was the country, indeed the world was still plunged into the worst depression since the 1930s. 54-year-old men were very low on any one's priorities to give jobs to, especially those that had a penchant for sailing off into the blue. To keep busy and save myself from daytime television, I agreed to be the Bosun at our yacht club (Thurrock) this is a purely volunteer post, no pay apart from a rare tip from some grateful member. My duties included checking and replacing the mooring gear, this invariably took place in the early morning, it was cold muddy and back breaking work. Luckily we had a good work boat, and my assistant Dave (pigtail) kept our moral up with constant funny banter.

However, people wanted to know how the Caribbean adventure with Gloria had panned out. So I set to work writing it up, over a couple of months, sitting on the sofa in the evening, while Helen watched East Enders and Coronation Street, a sort of book emerged. I say sort of, as even I could see that the grammar was not so good and the spelling was a bit weird, but I sent it over to a mate of mine who had self-published several books and had mentioned that he would help get mine published if I wrote one. Martin Bailey was as true as his word and in short order it was in the correct "format", several adjustments were made and just after Christmas a box arrived with four copies in it. The book "The boat they laughed at" was in existence! I cannot tell you the strange emotions that swept over me when I held it. I signed the first one and gave it to Helen. It was the first time she had read it, she had tried several times but she would go and point out "you cannot start a sentence with but" and I would say something rude and we would both sulk for a few days. In order that we did not stab each other I did not let her read it until the completed thing was in her hand.

The Excel boat show was on and I went there with Helen, we met up with Dick Durham and Edmund Whelan, I gave those three people copies, Dick Durham because he's a very good mate he has written several very good books, and I always enjoy what he writes in Yachting Monthly, but he insisted on paying me for it. And Edmund Whelan because he had egged me on and joined me for the first Atlantic crossing, a better companion for a hare-brained enterprise you could not ask for, always in a good mood, a fountain of knowledge, and generally one of the best. Martin Bailey was there too, so he had a book as well, and I had run out.

A bigger box was on order, and lots of people wanted them. Which was lucky, by selling books I just about kept the wolves from the door. I was gladdened that all the people who read it said how much they enjoyed it. I was even asked to give a short talk at Thurrock Yacht Club. I had been a member there for almost twenty one years. The talk was tacked onto a "Bern's night "celebration and we all had a good time, Ken Browning had put a number of our photos into PowerPoint presentation. He had the button, and had slipped in a picture of me working on my all over tan and took great delight on not moving on when I asked him too, the rascal. Edmund even managed to make to the event, it so we had a little reunion.

Roy Hart another Battlesbridge resident long distance sailor and the owner of the famous yacht "Victory" (she was an American cup challenger, almost, De Savery had two made and chose her sister ship for the important races, and maybe would have done better to have used the one Roy has) approached me soon after, he had enjoyed the book as well and asked if I would do a talk to the "old Gaffers association". Of course I agreed, and a date was set in March.

Gloria at rest at Battlesbridge. Picture by a kind gentleman called Jim whose surname escapes me.

Chapter 2

The night arrived, the talk was at the "Royal Burnham Yacht Club" It's a really posh good looking club, lots of wood panelling and pictures and half models of notable yachts. The room quickly filled up with "Old Gaffers" these people are pretty formidable, you meet them individually and you know you are in the presence of eccentricity, but as a group it's almost a riot! I had a lot of friends there, apart from Helen, Dick and Kathy Durham who had shown up (and I was always glad to see them), Roy Hart of course, and I saw Michael Peyton, the famous cartoonist lurking about the place as well. But I had bad nerves, I felt like a real outsider, and I needed something to break the ice. Just before I went on, inspiration struck!

Some years before I had been renting a Dutch barge at Battlesbridge, Gabriel the owner kept insisting I take it out for a spin one day. One fine summer's weekend coincided with a very good tide, since a few weeks previously with the help of local boatman "dodgy Dave" we had dried the barge out in the middle of the river on a patch of gravel and I had been able to check things like the rudder and prop out. Apart from having to replace a pin in the prop everything looked well enough for a quite trip down the river and back, I even uttered the fatal words, "What could possibly go wrong?" And invited my mother to join, myself, Dodgy and Peter who has another Dutch barge called "Hazel May" at Battlesbridge on a short jolly to Frambridge and back.

That morning the sun shone and the birds sang, even the old Deutz diesel started with ease, the barge floated two hours before high water, we sprang off, and only mildly crushing the dinghy alongside plodded along with a song in our hearts. Around the first bend I saw an old gaff rigged yacht aground in the channel, I managed to slide through the mud and get past. And then there was another to dodge. I was kept very busy at the wheel, the old barge had some very peculiar habits and a reluctance to go where I pointed her, but she did have a good turn of speed, and the engine sounded nice. About a mile further down the river widened, I took the opportunity to get better acquainted with the steering characteristics of the barge, hard to Port, then hard to Starboard, but then the steering went very oddly light, I put the gear selector in neutral and went and looked over the stern, there was a gaping gap where before a rudder had resided.

My mother asked me what the problem was, "rudder is gone " I said " what does that mean" she retorted, several pithy remarks came to mind but I settled on " we cannot steer". " how are you going to get us back then? " she asked, with rising panic "have a little faith " I replied. Peter suggested ramming the barge into the bank and coming back later when the tide had fallen to find the rudder and reattach it, not an idea that I favoured, because we were close to a large caravan site and I had visions of my home being stripped by wreckers while I was away organizing welders and such like. Dodgy waved down a passing motor boat and had them to take a tow rope, but as soon as we started moving the motor boat could not steer us and we almost rammed the bank anyway, I thanked them but had to ask them to disconnect in case there was an accident. Peter suggested using the dinghy with the out board to pull the head around, but the outboard was only 2 hp and the barge displaced about 100 tonnes, so it was too much of a struggle.

A bright idea was needed, and the old light bulb flashed on in my head, "The mast"!!! I rustled up some spanners and we unbolted the mast, it was only about twenty foot long and quite a light spar, using it we were able to push off the bank, get the barge headed in the right direction then give it a gentle kick ahead to get it moving slowly, between that and the tide that was still making, we gently made our way up the twisty channel to home. Flushed with success I had forgotten something, all those gaff rigged boats, some more had passed us and I had not noticed. We rounded last bend, it had all been going well up until that point, sadly the river gets a bit deeper and wider there and I failed to find anything to push against so we arrived sideways.

The pool before the bridge seemed to be full of varnished long bow sprits and much cherished wooded boats. The Old Gaffers Association had picked that particular day to have a club run to Battlesbridge. A sea of white faces stared unbelievingly as Peter attempted to get a rope ashore using the dinghy, the tide had almost slacked completely and if we did not do it then we would have swung across the fairway. I had horrible visions of getting stuck, blocking the channel and the barge breaking its back, luckily I managed to get a boot on a boat that was close to the stern and pushed off, the shore rope was connected to the other bank and suddenly, disaster was adverted and the barge was safely back in its berth.

So recalling this incident, my first words were, "Hi my name is Max Liberson, recently I returned from the Caribbean in a Ferro schooner, now moored at Battlesbridge, but before I tell you about it I find I must apologise to you, we have met before" the talking died down people started to pay attention, I outlined the above incident, or attempted to, halfway through a lady shouted out "it was you!" and the joint collapsed with laughter! Ice has not been broken like that since the Titanic crunched her way through her plates on a cold night in 1912.

The evening was a great success, I had some books to sell, and one I gave to be raffled. A lady I vaguely recognised won it and later on she came up to me and said "I am reading your book, the grammars appalling, the spelling not very good, but I am loving it!" What I did not know was this lady was the wife of Mike Peyton, her name is Kath, she is a very prolific writer and has had at least fifty books published. Not to mention a series that aired on BBC television some years ago.

Chapter 3

Some weeks later, Roy Hart called me up and told me to ring Kath, I did and she asked me to come and see her. I and Helen went. It's always good to see Mike I had been to see him before. As well as being an extraordinary artist he can tell you tales that will raise the hairs on the back of your neck. His war time experiences were like something out of a nightmare. He joined the 8th army, lied about his age to get in, fought in the desert, was taken prisoner by the Italians, shipped to Italy, and then moved to Germany. He escaped several times, the last time he avoided re-capture. Then he and his mate joined the Red army and fought their way back across Europe until he met up with his own regiment. When he tells you these things he does it in a 'matter of fact' Yorkshire way like it was an everyday event. He is a very modest man and probably won't thank me for writing this, but it's the truth and I think he should be regarded as a national treasure.

But we were there to see Kath. She told me she had liked my book so much she had sent it to her published "Adlar Coles" I was astounded! We had a very enjoyable afternoon, talking about this and that. And meeting one of their daughters, it was difficult to leave later, but we did.

In between the talks, and book selling the mud awaited. We worked hard, and were getting though the moorings when I had a problem with another committee member. It was all very petty and stupid, but the situation just got worst and worst with his friends on the committee hinting that I should go because I was "bringing the club into disrepute", and generally making things difficult for me as Bosun, all because I would not turn a blind eye to this behaviour. I had been a member of the club for twenty one years was proud of that fact, but TYC began to lose its charm for me. I felt like a mug, knocking myself out for no pay, crawling around in the cold Thames mud, for very little thanks. Something I had been quite happy to do in the past, but now because of inter club politics I began to question why I was there. Suddenly it was like a love affair that had gone wrong, you know one day you look at a woman and she is beautiful, the next day because of something, the woman looks unattractive. It's the same woman, but something inside dies and that's how I felt about my club. It was a shame, I had had some very good times in the club and there were and still are some very good people there, but for me the magic had vanished. All that was left was unpaid drudgery.

Chapter 4

I was still looking for some kind of work and a friend called Graham Smith said he would send an e mail to one of the bigger delivery companies to try and get me some. It seemed to get a result, because one Thursday morning I was the down the yacht club, wondering where the next bit of money was going to come from. My phone rang and I answered it, "Hi N...here, I received Graham's e mail, I have a Sun Fast 37 that has to be taken from Portsmouth to Gothenburg, are you up for it? When has it got to be there I asked, "Yesterday, I have been let down" N replied. From long experience I have learnt that most things can be worked out, so I said "yes, ok, I can be there tomorrow morning". Then N... said, great, what about crew? "Ah, do you have anyone?" I asked, "Yes one person, I will get them down, find someone else." He replied. We talked money, it was not very lucrative, however it was work and I could not afford to be choosey. I looked around the club, Mick Newman was on the balcony drinking tea, and I asked him, "Fancy a sail to Sweden?" He looked at me saw I was serious, and said "yes". I don't know who was more surprised. "How long will it take us do you think?" he asked. "About a week I hope." I told him. He made a few phone calls and I arranged to meet him at Grays train station the next morning.

I saw my mate Peter and got him to drive me over to Battlesbridge to Gloria to collect my sailing gear and go over to the caravan to see what North Sea charts I had. We took this to my partner Helen's house in Basildon, then we went back to the yacht club so I could hand over my responsibilities as club Bosun to various people. It was the busiest timeout the year in the Bosun's office; we had the Port of London Authority coming over to check the outer trot moorings, and then the week after that the big crane was due to lift the yachts in for the start of the season. The lads were understanding. I passed my keys over to Chris and my assistant Dave promised to keep things going. So I left for the 12-mile pedal home to Basildon and Helen.

I phoned N.., for some more details told him the happy news about the crew I had, and then I went online to do some research. The weather looked good if we moved fast. There had been some lovely weather the last week, but the bad stuff was coming. How-ever if we could get above the Wash and the wind went N.W. like my forecast said then we might get a cracking fast sail all the way to the Kattegat.

N ran a delivery company that in the past I had tried to get into. I knew he had a lot of work; if I could impress him then it could lead to good things. Needless to say I did not sleep so well that night. Helen took me to the train station at Pitsea the next morning and I boarded the train to Grays. It was with not a small amount of relief that I saw Mick waiting for me with a huge holdall at his feet. Mick is about the same age as me (mid-fifties) and although not a big bloke he is a real biker and always has a smile on his face. I paid for our tickets to Portsmouth and not long after we were on the train.

The trip to Portsmouth took a few hours, but it was a pleasant journey, England was in the throes of spring, the sun was out and people seemed happy around us. Finally we arrived at the yacht and made contact with the broker. He showed us over the vessel, telling us it had been a school boat over the last 10 years. She had led a hard life, but mostly was all there, accept there was no storm jib and a battery was out. In fact, the battery had blown up and might have caught fire looking at the scorch marks on it and the surrounding woodwork. The broker said there was a new battery fitted, but apart from that it was "sold as seen".

Mick and I rolled up our sleeves and started work, firstly on a shopping list, and then checking things over, items like gas and what all the switches did. I was a bit disconcerted to note that there was no heater, spray hood or an auto pilot. We pulled the mainsail out and put the reefs in, at least there was three slabs. Sadly, no lazy jacks were rigged from the mast to the boom, so getting a good reef in was going to be a difficult job shorthanded. I also took the jib from the fore cabin and hoisted it in the furling gear. It went up ok, but when I tried to furl it, turns were pulled into the top of the forestay, jamming everything and forcing me to go up in a Bosun's chair to sort out the mess. I dropped it on the foredeck and lashed it to the rails. It was quite a small jib, so we would just have to have it either up or down. We went to the supermarket and bought food, enough for six days. And the day light was fading. I phoned the third hand, and discovered that it was a girl, and she had decided that a trip across the North Sea in early spring was not for her. I was not really surprised. It was going to be a difficult trip with just the two of us, no auto pilot, and a very exposed steering position, but Mick was up for it. We talked bikes for a while then went to bed, at least we each had a large aft cabin to ourselves, but bloody hell it was cold!

Mick Newman steering Yacht 53 towards Gothenburg

Chapter 5

The next morning, I checked the forecast, which was for Northerly winds. So I phoned N... and said "we are good to go, ok with you?" He gave me the good word, so I called up the lock, got the green light from them and we were off!

53 was soon clear of Portsmouth and headed east for the Looe channel. We had to do a few tacks and during one I heaved too so we could pump out the bilges because they had filled and there was a bit of water sloshing about (the bilge on the Sun Fast 37 are like most modern yachts not very deep it does not take much to fill them, water can build up in a locker and get displaced when the yacht is sailed for the first time so I was not unduly alarmed). It was cold but 53 was getting along nicely. There was however one little fly in the ointment. We noticed that without the engine running a weird "oooohing" noise would start up when the boat hit 5 knots, as the speed picked up the noise would get louder, at about 6 knots it was impossible to sleep in the after cabins, at 7 it was positively deafening! We traced the noise down to the prop "singing," it would make this noise even with the gear box engaged and the shaft locked and the prop not even turning. Now I don't know about you but whenever I have heard of singing props mentioned I sort of get an image of the Little mermaid crooning sweetly away, not the ear bashing screech that we were getting! 53 needed a new prop to fix this problem. During the night the cold was so intense that Mick and I stood hourly tricks at the wheel, the big stainless steel wheel. Even with gloved fingers it was painful to touch, and the decks became slippery with ice.

The dawn found us just past Dungeness, we had made fairly good time and were in a favourable tide stream that we could carry all the way to Ramsgate, but we had to use the motor during the night so I wanted to stop and top up the tank. Normally I would have gone to Neuport in Belgium but the situation with red diesel and the British yachts that had been fined for having it in their tanks decided me against a stop there. As we entered Ramsgate I put the gear box into neutral and gave it a bit of astern, then tried to engage ahead again, it would not go in and made some very worrying noises. We were slowly moving ahead so I put alongside a yacht already in the fuel berth and stopped her with ropes.

My first though was that the gearbox was blown. On further investigation and with some help from the people on the yacht we had tied up to, it appeared that it was just excessive play on the gear change. With the other crew fending us off, we backed out of the fuel berth and onto and empty finger pontoon. We then went into town to get some tools, grease and oil. While there we had lunch in a café - it was good to get off the yacht. Back on board we carefully dismantled the Morse control box, adjusted the cables, and lubricated everything. Somebody had been in the box before and failed to replace the rubber gasket properly; sea water had been washing the insides ever since. That job took up quite a bit of time, but at least it seemed to fix the gear change problem. I pumped out the bilges again while I was at it. I had to admit that we had a small leak from somewhere. However, I could not track it down. We were both tired from the night before so I told Mick that we would fuel up and leave in the morning, I hated missing the weather that was sunny with a good northerly wind, but I knew that with just the two of us exhaustion was a bigger barrier to a successful conclusion to the trip than almost anything else.

We slept well and topped up the fuel tank with 60 litres at 07.00 hrs the next morning, then we put to sea, once clear of the wind farms we pointed 53's bows to the North East, hardened up the sheets and she dug her shoulder in and started to romp, accompanied by a dreadful caterwauling from aft! Sadly, the wind faded later and we had to restart the motor to keep up the 5-6 knots I wanted, the 30hp yanmar diesel only needed a tad over 2000 revs to keep this speed, so I did not think it was using much fuel.

The next problem then showed up, the FM/LW radio would not pick up BBC radio 4 as soon as we got offshore, so without the radio I could not get a forecast. This was annoying because the last report I had at Ramsgate was that the weather situation was going to deteriorate. I had a solution to that, apart from just relying on the barometer that had started to drop pretty much from when we left harbour. My cunning plan was to go and find an oil rig. It's been my experience in the past that calling up the oil rig's guard ship on VHF invariably results in a deafening silence. They don't answer, however if a guard ship thinks you're going to come closer to the oil rig than the allowed 3 cables he will make contact to remind you of the rules, at which point you can ask for the latest forecast. That's how I found out that there was a N.E. gale on its way! I was not surprised, as I said we had lost rather a lot of milli bars on the barometer over the last 12 hours or so. But what to do? I decided that with the leak, lack of storm sails, dodgy gear box and lack of crew we were not up to a North sea gale, the nearest safe haven was Terschilling, almost dead to windward, So we altered course for there, I attempted to take down the fore sail, but halfway down it jammed, so I lashed it around the forestay, then flattened out the main sail and with the engine chugging away below, we made good progress.

The low lying land reluctantly showed just before we lost the last of the daylight, with our hearts in our mouths we closed with the starboard hand marker buoy that, once identified, put us in the channel that would take us into the harbour. Not before time either, as the rain was slashing down and the wind was building with every gust. The ebbing tide was ripping out bringing our speed over the ground down to 3 knots. Finally, after several long cold hours of darkness and rain we made it to where I thought the entrance was, we identified the Port and Starboard hand lights, just as the Reeds said they would be, but it looked like they marked a solid wall. To make things even more interesting a three knot current hammered across the channel. I balanced our speed and course to keep us on station, then wound her up, offsetting our course to allow for drift, and charged at the black hole. Mick was sure we would crash. We didn't, and emerged into the perfect tranquillity of a harbour, fast as you like we tied up to a pontoon, and Mick put the kettle on. We had a cup of tea, something to eat and hit the sack.

Mick slept well. My sleeping bag was not warm enough to allow me to get a proper kip despite turning in fully clothed. Deciding to get a better one later that day, I attempted to get at least some rest. Our first priority in the morning after breakfast was to re-plan the route. I had wanted to go outside of Denmark, up the North Sea, which was the passage I had done in the past and I had charts for. Now I realised that the more sheltered route of the Kiel Kanal and the Baltic would be a better if slower way to Gothenburg. After eating, Mick and I went over to the harbourmaster's office, where I paid for two nights stay and he allowed me to access my e mails and print off some documents. I asked him about charts, to which he said a shop in town might be able to help.

Chapter 6

Mick and I went back to 53 and sorted out the forestay furling gear. It was only a screw that had worked itself loose that was jamming the sail up, so I soon sorted that out. Then we put the sail cover on the main, not bothering to take our waterproofs and boots off, instead walking into town with them on. The rain continued to fall out the grey sky like it was never going to stop. The chart shop did not have the charts we needed, and the local super market only sold insipid weak tea bags. We did how ever get a jar of stock powder that could be made into a warming drink. After some other grocery shopping we moved on to the camping shop, looking for a thicker sleeping bag for me. They had a sleeping bag, but it was another "summer" weight one, so I bought it as at least it was big enough that I could put my other one inside it. We spotted a place to eat that night and then went back to the boat.

There was a Swedish yacht moored close to us, while I was stowing the grub, Mick went for shower and then met the Swedes, returning to tell me that they had charts. I wasted no time and paid them a visit. The skipper was called Anders. He did have some charts, but not all the way up to where we had to go, and looking at all the rocks and islands I realised that the Baltic was no place to skimp on charts.

Back on number"53" we waited for the rain to stop. It didn't so I cooked up another stew and we had an early night. In my double sleeping bags I was wonderfully comfy and warm and had a superb sleep for a change. In the morning the rain had stopped, the wind had gone around to the North; it was colder, but brighter. We made ready for sea. I wanted to get some more fuel, but the pumps were conspicuous by their absents and the fuel gauge said we had a half a tank left so I thought we had enough anyway, and we left.

It took some time to clear the estuary, then when we turned North East we could not quite make our course, there was a bit of a sea running and the tide was against us as well. Progress was slow, even with the engine running at low revs. This was a problem because I wanted to get in the Elbe in time to catch the whole flood up to Cuxhaven, and time was tight. I was hopeful that the wind would back and we would get a Westerly breeze to help us like the forecast I saw on the harbourmaster's notice board suggested. Timing is everything and we did not have it that trip; the wind was on the nose for the first 15 hours or so. "53" was lovely, fast and fairly close winded, given the state of her mainsail, however the tacking we had to do was dropping our speed made good considerably. Then the wind died completely. We motored until the dawn, then gradually our longed-for Westerly started to build. The sea in the entrance of the Elbe was very lumpy and confused. We had the whole main out and were running. I rigged a preventer on the main boom and in the absence of a spinnaker pole to keep the sails clew out I had to drop the foresail; the constant filling and banging about was not doing the poor thing any good at all. About mid-morning an awkward sea hit "53"s big stern, she span around and we gybed big time, the preventer did its work, and probably saved the mast. I did not want a repeat performance so I took the main down completely, under bare poles we were still making 4 knots through the water, I started up the engine again and at a little more than tick-over we were up to 6 knots, with another 2 or so of tide to help us. I would have re hoisted the fore sail, but it was a two handed job, and someone had to steer with the confused sea, someone had to be on the wheel the whole time. I realised my mistake a few hours later. The fuel gauge suddenly started to drop into the last quarter, according to my calculations we should have had about 30 litres left, easily enough to make the 15 miles to Cuxhaven, but then the tide turned, (it runs hard in the Elbe, up to five knots off Cuxhaven). Our progress slowed. By myself I managed to reef the big mainsail down to the third row and hoisted it while Mick steered. As the daylight started to fade, "53" leaned from the wind and the motor started to suck air because of low fuel level. We could not go back, into the maelstrom that was now the entrance of the Elbe. With a dying engine it would have been the height of folly for a stranger to attempt to sail into Cuxhaven with a tide of up to 5 knots across the entrance, in the dark. The only alternative was to anchor, and I saw a possible place. It was outside the channel and sheltered by a training wall, Mick helmed us in and when he told me the depth was down to 5 meters I told him to bring us into the wind and as the way came off I dropped the anchor, which bit straight away. I got the sail off and the black ball out, then we found the all-round white light, and got that rigged as well. The rain had turned to wet sleet by then. Finally, we could have a cup of tea and sort out our next move. I radioed up the Cuxhaven VTS (Vessel Transit Service) on channel 71 to advise them of our actions. The guy I spoke to asked if we needed anything "some diesel would be nice" I quipped, to my astonishment I heard a voice say " I'll do that" The VTS told me a boat would show up soon with the diesel. I was very impressed, it was a filthy night, very cold, very wet and the wind was building still.

Chapter 7

A small motor boat with the letters SAR plastered down the side made an appearance soon after, it came alongside and I took the proffered bow rope. After the greetings, I was offered a container of diesel, "that's great, can I buy that?" I asked "No" said the skipper. I began to get worried, "ok sir, as you can see, we are safely anchored in sheltered water, do you agree?" The skipper smiled and said "sure, put the diesel in your tank". I did, and noticed it was red diesel. It turns out, that was why I could not buy it. Once I was convinced that we were not going to get a massive bill I gave the skipper 90 euros (all we had in cash aboard the yacht) for coming out on such a nasty night. They stood by while we extracted the anchor and got underway.

While I went below to check on the course to Cuxhaven, Mick made a mistake, which was entirely understandable in the circumstances, and we strayed into the big ship channel. I came up and steered to put us back in our proper place. As it was raining hard I had put the wash board back in and we did not hear the radio. Cuxhaven VTS was calling us up; I found that out because the next thing that happened was a big patrol boat showed up and a put a search light on us. We were told off and also told that they would be following us to Cuxhaven. As we arrived off there another smaller police boat took over and ordered us to follow them in. We were soon tied up in a marina. The police came aboard and asked where the rest of the crew was. I told him that it was just me and Mick. We all went below where it was damp and very cold rather than wet and very cold topsides. The police man shivered "you have no heater?" "No, and no auto pilot either" I said. He said, "What was your last port?" I told him Tschelling, he looked at us, both obviously very cold wet and tired and said "Okay, you broke the law when you came into the big ship channel, and I have to give you a fine, but we make it a small fine". The next hurdle was then reached; I had given all our euros as a tip to the men who had brought the diesel out to us, but that was easily solved - the policeman radioed for a car to take me to a cash point. I think that must have been the most expensive 15 euros that the police have ever collected, two boats, a car and goodness knows how many policemen, but they certainly made their point.

Once the police had left I put the dinner on. It was so cold that we did not bother to change out of our wet weather gear, even keeping our gloves on. Mick tried to butter a piece of bread but the butter was rock hard and just destroyed the bread, "think I will leave it out the ice box (that had no ice in it) tonight "He said with a straight face. We were still chuckling about that when we turned in (fully dressed) to get some well needed sleep.

As soon as the office opened in the morning we paid at the yacht club for our stay of two nights, and walked into town to look for charts of the Baltic. We found a shop that stocked them, but only in big portfolios, I would have needed two to cover all the area I needed and they were outrageously expensive. We wandered around a bit and had our photo taken with some people dressed as Vikings, or maybe Vikings from another era transported to down town Cuxhaven - it was hard to tell. We did some food shopping and I tried to find an internet café. Not being able to, I phoned Helen and asked her to go into my e mails and find the details of a German friend Martin, who lived in Hamburg. If there was no phone number she could e mail him and ask for one.

Later that night I had a phone call from Martin. It was good to catch up. Even better, he agreed to lend me the charts I would need, and suggested meeting in Kiel in a couple of days. Sorted!

Chapter 8

We still had gearbox problems, but we managed to limp into the Kiel Kanal's lock gates the next day. But there the gearbox would not go into ahead from neutral. After paying the very modest fee to transit this remarkable bit of engineering, I disconnected the gear shift, and put the gearbox lever into ahead. This meant we had no astern but at least we would have drive when we started the engine.

Although we were the first boat in the lock I waved the other vessels past, and gave them a good head start before we left. I did not want to be having to do anything quickly that might involve going astern, because we couldn't!

The day passed pleasantly, it was even warmish, and for once the rain had stopped as we meandered along, after filling up with diesel not long after leaving the lock gates. That night we were going to have to stop, because traffic is not allowed to transit after dark. We were about halfway along but I could not see where the stopping place was. So I radioed up Kiel Kanal control, I was told that I could stop at the next turnoff (which was a side canal) but I did not need to go into the canal. The next branch-off duly appeared, and we went a little way into it but could not see any place to tie up. So we turned around and went back to the main waterway where there where some big Dolphins for ships to moor to. I decided to treat them as pile moorings and gently nosed up to the first one, Mick (a tree surgeon in the real world) leap onto it, scaled it, and I passed him a long mooring rope that he fed into a ring and passed back. We did the same to the one astern and in short order we were securely moored fore and aft between the two huge dolphins. I had just got the dinner on when Mick called me up, a car ferry was alongside, the skipper told me I could not moor where we were and I should follow him into the side canal. We got un-moored, very easily and duly followed the car ferry. Coming around a bend further along than we had travelled, I then understood the directions - there was a set of canal gates, and just before that several yachts had already moored up, Doh! Soon we were enjoying a very peaceful dinner, in very tranquil surroundings.

The next morning, we were late getting going, all the other yachts had gone, and it was raining again, as well as being bitterly cold. We continued our trip, and I got to thinking that soon we would be in the area that my father was stationed just after the way; I know he had fond memories of the place. I did not see much to recommend it, but perhaps it's better in the sunshine. Every now and then a big ship would pass. It was tempting to get right over out of the way, but you have to be careful in case the ships wash pushes you into the stony bank. Several larger yachts passed us and we envied them their spray hoods that they invariably sported; very big structures they tended to be too. We also seemed to be a lot slower than most as well, judging by the way they came blasting past.

Martin called up from time to time to ask where we were. Then suddenly we rounded the last bend and could see the lock gates, and what an impressive piece of engineering they are too. I can see that it must have been a big day in German history when they were opened.

I called up the lock keeper and he told us we would have to wait for a short time, but it was not long before we were invited in. I had to tell him that we would come in slowly because we had no astern. Slowly we crept in and then Martin appeared with his son, Lassi, who I had not met before. He very obligingly caught our stern rope and braked us by dropping a turn around a cleat. We shook hands while the lock keeper emptied the lock and dropped us down to the level of the water outside the lock. Martin suggested I tie up at the little marina just to Port as we exited the lock, which we did.

Chapter 9

I put the kettle on and Martin came aboard with a small mountain of charts for us to borrow. Then he started hiding small chocolate Easter eggs around the boat while his son was fishing off the cockpit. Martin noticed how cold it was below and was shocked when I told him we had no heater. We went over the best route for us to get to Bua near Gothenburg. Sadly, it was not past "Middle fart" I am juvenile enough to have wanted to go there because of the name. He also told me to be very careful to not go into the shipping lanes because the German police would give us a very big fine if we did, not a little 15 euro one like in the Elbe. Once we had sorted that out we went for a Pizza. A very fine one it was too! It was good to catch up with him. He had sold his beautiful yacht and bought the house of his dreams and was busy fixing it up. Much too soon it was time to go back to yacht 53 and try and catch some sleep. The forecast was for more rain, with Martin noting that it was the worst Easter in living memory.

Morning was grey and the sky pregnant with bulging rain clouds, we found the showers. They only had cold water. Suitably refreshed I returned to the yacht. We went food shopping at a nearby super market and finished off our Euros in a sausage shop. I asked for a selection, and we were given a large bag of mixed produce. The only dark moment came when Mick asked if they had any Polish sausage. We managed to exit before we became part of the next batch.

I paid our mooring fee (5 euros including the cold water shower) and we left. There was a gentle wind once away from the bank, and we could just about make our course. We stood two hour tricks at the wheel, were careful of the shipping lanes and soon were of passing part of Denmark and weaving through small angling boats.

Night came, the visibility dropped to very bad with a patchy fog and light, cold rain. We had to get under a road bridge after dog legging through a channel. I had found the right channel but when we got to the bridge we were both very doubtful if we could get under it. I re-checked the chart for about the third time. In the end I called up the coast guard, he confirmed that we would fit. We still held our breaths as we went through. It was a long night, but as usual dawn did eventually reluctantly turn blackness into grey. I had said we might spend a night at an island, but I found I was loathe to stop. If we cracked on we could be in Bua that evening. It was time to crack on, not skulk in ports. The wind obliged by going up to about a force 6, I got the big reef in, and yacht 53 started singing her favourite song - well her banshee wail anyhow! Seriously, in the flat water, hard on the wind she became a joy to steer, if not trying to sleep down below, and was soon hitting close to 9 knots, wonderful sailing!

Chapter 10

As the evening came the wind dropped off. We were sailing slower and with full sail up when my phone rang. It was my boss asking where we were. I told him, and he said he wanted to arrange my next delivery. He asked me if I wanted to take a brand new 45 yacht to Turkey. I said "sure" and he replied that I deserved a treat after the trip I had just had.

We closed the little fishing port of Bua and in the last of the daylight doglegged around the channel and moored up to a quiet peaceful jetty where several other yachts were tied up. I slept very well that night, content that we had done a good job despite the leak, gearbox problems, undermanned, with some very nasty weather we had safely delivered the yacht.

Cleaning began early, first with the yacht and then with ourselves. I rang up to find out who was going to accept the yacht. There was a problem - the owners were not expecting us and could not get down until the week end. I was told to take lots of photos and leave the keys with the harbourmaster. There were no keys... I wrote a letter to the new owner and remembered to connect the gearbox up, to prevent any accidents. Then we gave all the food left over to an appreciative old man and went off to catch a plane back to U.K. We had to catch a bus, then a train and finally another bus that took us to the airport. There I was very happy to find that the airline accepted payment on my credit card for our tickets. While we waited Mick bought us a beer each, for £14!!!!

Then I looked up and saw the tall figure of Tom Cunliffe (yacht journalist, writer and legendary yachtsman) making his way through the crowds. I called out to him and we had a chat. He asked us what we were doing, I told him and he said "it's nice to meet some proper sailors" which I thought was very good of him to say. The flight did not take long and very soon we were suffering on the London Underground.

Back in the U.K. life was not so much fun, I was still scratching around for bits of work while being the unpaid club Bosun at TYC. Obviously I had made enemies by not turning a blind eye to a committee member helping himself to diesel and attempting to get him slung out. We (me and my assistant Dave) struggled on but there was constant bickering and games. I was more than happy to get another phone call from N asking if I could deliver a 45-foot brand new Lagoon catamaran to Split. I said I would make some calls. My first was to Helen, to see if she would come. I told her it was a dream job, a bit of luxury in a brand new yacht, going to a place in the sun, and even getting paid a little for it, what more could you want? As it turned out I was a bit wide of the mark. Helen said "yes." I phoned Mick and asked him if he would come to, he also agreed to be part of the crew, so there was three of us. I phoned N back and told him we were on and he asked that we get to La Corunna by Thursday to meet the yacht that was being sailed there by its owner. That was not possible, but we managed to get there on Friday, only one date late. We arrived there at Corunna marina at 21.00 hrs and found the yacht, all locked up. So we went off for a meal and came back later, it was still locked up. I called the Boss and asked him for instructions, he told me to meet up with another skipper who was working for the same firm as me delivering the same model of Catamaran, and he said if it came to it he would find some space on his yacht so we could get out of the rain at least. Then the Russian owner of the Lagoon we were to deliver came back. There were five in his crew, and it seemed they had been having a party since arriving in Spain. He gave me some very quick instructions regarding the boat, and then dropped a bombshell - the auto pilot had died. A new pump was on its way but would take a week to get delivered. I could stay with the Lagoon in La Corunna and wait for it, or move on to further down the coast, the choice was mine. After that I left to get some sleep after agreeing to meet him at 05.00 to collect the papers and keys before he left for St Petersburg in the morning.

Chapter 11

Over a beer back on the other Lagoon, the fellow skipper gave me a few tips on handling the big cat. He said it could take bad weather, but to treat it more as a motor-sailer. Also, worryingly he said he would not consider moving it without an auto pilot or a much bigger crew than I had because it was a bitch to steer. After a cup of tea Helen and I went to our cabin to try and get some sleep. It was a long night, my new skipper chum had turfed one of his crew out of his cabin to give it to me and Helen. Said crew were miffed and all night long kept getting up and stomping about, and it was a relief to get out of bed at 05.00 and go and see the Russian owner. The party had been going all night and was still in full swing when I got there, while they were packing they were still downing shots! The owner gave me 100 euros towards the extra marina costs, showed me the papers then while I was not looking put them back in his briefcase and left.

This is not how a text book handover is supposed to take place. I was expecting to go over a detailed list of what was on the yacht and what was damaged. Instead I had been shown (only because I asked) how the generator started, he had said the Genoa was difficult to furl, and that the mainsail cover was torn. And that was that. My crew started to turn up and Helen, god bless her, started to clean up. Mick wondered around with his jaw dragging in amazement at our new toy.

I could see his point, the Lagoon 450 is a big beast and very posh with a staircase up to the "flying bridge", acres of white glass fibre set off with sparkling stainless steel and neat trims of teak. Helen was well impressed when she found the dishwasher, but less so when the mussels in the freezer where discovered, (they were quite old). Mick and I started checking things out. The Lagoon we had stayed on the night before was leaving to catch a weather window. I wished we could have left at the same time - it goes against the grain to lose a fair wind, but I had to find out more about the auto pilot situation and get to know the boat, apart from all the provisioning that had to be done.

We stayed a couple of days. It should have been longer, but under the terms of the contract I had signed I had to pay up front for the marina charges and be reimbursed eventually at the end of the delivery, as the rate for a large Cat was running at 45 euros per day I simply did not have the finances available to stay there as well as funding the rest of the trip. As well as the financial worries both of my crew only had 3 weeks available to be absent from their normal lives. At that point I should have renegotiated my contract but as I had already dipped into the funds given to me up front to pay for the air tickets and other expenses I felt somewhat duty bound to carry on and somehow get the boat to Croatia.

Looking at the forecast I could see that if we left on the third day we would have a light south-westerly to begin with and then a stronger westerly at the latter part of the day. The winds would continue to increase but I thought we could find some sheltered anchorage if we had to the next day, and that would not cost me anything. As I was looking at the charts I noticed that the original papers the owner had shown me where missing, so I called him up. He looked in his briefcase and found them, but he was then home in St Petersburg! He sent copies of them on an e mail for me to print off. I went up to the marina office and spoke to the girl there, she printed off the copies and contacted the yachts builder and arranged for our new auto pilot pump to be shipped to a Spanish port 120 miles before Gibraltar. I then paid for our stay and returned to the yacht.

So we left, and at least I impressed Helen by not crashing as we exited. Once clear of the harbour collision alarms started going off on the bridge, but as the chart plotter instructions were all in Russian it took a few goes to switch them off. We then hoisted the big roached mainsail and motored into the calm sea. At first all seemed wonderful, the yacht was a pleasure to steer in the gentle conditions even if the topside steering position was very exposed. Later the wind picked up and the cat became increasingly difficult to keep on course. There was no feedback through the wheel, and no directional stability, once she started to veer off course the helmsman had to apply lots of helm the other way to correct it, then as the yacht came back to the course, she would keep going and the helmsman would have to apply more helm but the other way. To add to the frustration, the steering was very heavy. After a short stint on the wheel, my arms started to ache, and Helen did not have enough muscle to steer at all in the prevailing conditions. I could see why the auto pilot had died. The next ominous revelation came when I turned off the engine and we sailed. Or seemed to, I was horrified at how much leeway we were making, the yacht pointed up okay, but our track over the ground was far from reasonable, I tried reefing the main, that made things a bit better but still our track made good was more like my old Ferro schooner's than half a millions euros' worth of catamaran. We were moving along nicely, just not in the right direction. As the night descended Mick and Helen went down with mal de mare. The seas got bigger and it rained hard.

Chapter 12

Off Finisterre in the early hour of the morning I attempted to put the last reef in the main. I was tired, the wind was suddenly starting to blow up to the high 30 knots and I made a mistake; the other two reefs had gone in on a single line, the sail cover masked the third reef at the mast. I did not know that this one had to be put in by hand after climbing some way up the mast. Slacking of the mainsail halyard, I took up the slack in the third reefing line, once that was tight, I tensioned up the halyard, but something did not look right, so I climbed the mast and found that by not putting in the luff reef by hand I had torn a small hole in the brand new sail. I then stowed all the sail, with difficulty because the Genoa would not roll away, and we motored. However, we had to slow right down or the yacht would slam horribly. A haven was needed, and I found a small bay on the chart which we headed for. We reached there in the daylight of a stormy morning, the bay I wanted to anchor in was full of fishing gear, but finally at the end of it I found space. It was a bit deep at 10 meters but beggars can't be choosers, and I got our ground tackle ready. The big delta was attached to 80 metres of 12 mm chain according to the manual, so I had high hopes of its efficiency, these were sadly dashed when I started to let the chain out and found there was only 20 meters of chain. There was 60 meters of heavy nylon anchor rode however so I let that all out. Then I made a howling error. We were in effect on a lee shore now because there was a beach behind us (as well as one in front) I wanted to get maximum rode down. Because at the end of the day the efficiency of the ground tackle depends on length of rode, especially if rope is being used rather than chain. We could not take any chances of dragging. At the time it seemed the easiest way to make sure we had maximum scope out was to disconnect the bitter end (a big mistake) And connect it to the bridal ropes (that led to both hull's bows), I secured all with bowline knots, then I tied in a big mooring rope to the lot so we could haul it all back aboard. This gained us about 15 meters of much needed scope, which was an important consideration, but it also meant that when we did recover the gear we would have to disconnect it all at some point to get the bitter end back in the locker.

We laid there for two days and the wind howled up to 40 knots at times, it was not a lot of fun, but better than getting hammered outside. The owner called me up, and being the honest soul that I am I made the mistake of telling him I had torn his sail; he was not impressed and phoned my boss. My boss phoned me and wanted to know what was going on, after I told him what had happened he told me to get to Bayonna as fast as possible fix the damage and not to talk to the owner again. So later that day when the wind dropped down we started to recover the anchor. It came in easy, well for the first twenty foot anyway, the wind had dropped right off, and we were in danger of running over the anchor rode, so I took both the engines out of gear and rushed to help Mick, I disconnected the bridals and put the rode on the windlass drum with four turns, when suddenly a squall hit and the wind came back with a vengeance. The yacht began to sail, and when she brought up on the rode the strain of her 17 tons' weight moving at 4 knots started to turn the windless drum backwards. It was dragging my hands into the drum. When I let go, the miserable little preventer I had rigged snapped off (it was the only spare line on the yacht) and the anchor with all the chain and nylon rode, was gone! Helen was less than amused, and I was feeling sick. Mick had to be stopped from jumping after it. What could we do? There was no one about to ask for assistance, we had no other anchor deploy or use to try and drag for the lost gear, the daylight was fast fading. I decided we should go to Bayonna and sort things out there. Another long night followed, there was still a big sea running from the strong winds, and we could not push the cat because of the slamming, but we eventually arrived there in the next morning and tied up in the marina.

Chapter 13

Attending to the formalities I was pleasantly surprised when the lady in the office accepted our copied documents, after which I went looking first for a sail maker. No luck; the only one was miles away and first we would have to take the big sail off, take the battens out, arrange transport, get him to do it, then get it back. It looked like a long saga for such a small hole. I bought sail repair materials so we could do it ourselves. Then I looked for an anchor, I found a delta "type" that was not too horribly expensive and ordered it, apparently it would be there later that day. Next, I tried for 12mm chain, almost falling over when they told me the price per meter - 20 euros!!! I thought they were talking about stainless at first, but no, it really was 20 euros per meter of galvanised ordinary chain. I did not buy any. Along the street I found a shop that sold gear to the fishing boats, but unfortunately they did not have any chain but they did have some heavy nylon rope. I bought fifty meters of that. It was quite reasonable. Back at the yacht I and Mick sewed and patched the hole. It was not very big and all went back together well enough, in fact when it was up the mast it was very hard to see the repair at all.

Of course the anchor did not arrive, but it did the next morning, so we only had to pay for one night before we left. I sent a quick report on the sail damage did not bother to mention the anchor fiasco and "got the hell out of Dodge". Our next port of call was to be Cais Cais, near Lisbon. There I was instructed to report to the engine service place and have the engines serviced. We were having trouble with the chart plotter, being still in Russian, a language that I do not understand. Somewhere along the line I pressed a button that put all the lights out and we could not read it anymore. Good job I had paper charts that I had brought. Also the reefing lines were of such poor quality they were shredding all the time - if you left them in for more than a few hours the outer case would start breaking up and the line would no longer run through the blocks. Another major gripe was the problems we were having with furling the Genoa; sometimes it would but others not. We did manage to get to Cais Cais in a little over 30 hours. It was evening, so we anchored in the anchorage. I worried about how the new anchor would perform as it did not have any chain to help it. But it dug in well and we did not move during the night, unlike a small mono hull near us that had to keep resetting their pick several times.

The yacht had a nice little RIB and a big outboard, but without any petrol. So after placing it very carefully on the rib's transom I rowed it ashore to the marina with Mick and we went to the office to ask about charges. It was a posh office - marble floors and all that. The man there told me that for a cat of our size I would have to pay 50 euros per night, and add to that 25 euros' catamaran supplement, then add to that 25 percent tax. I thanked him and bid him goodbye while Mick used the toilet. We went off to find the engineer, but his office was shut. We left a message. On the way back I bought some petrol and we flew back across the sea to the yacht. Then I had a phone call from the owner. I told him where we were and he said we did not need to service the engines; it had been done already. I called my boss, who told me off for talking to the owner, then called me back to say we could go. I took Helen ashore for a walk and some food shopping. We had a nice look about, and stopped for a coffee, the bar we had stopped at had Wi-Fi so I found out the Russian word for the menu we needed to reset the chart plotter language to English. We stayed another night and left with a promise of Northerly winds, and would you believe it? They arrived! Soon the big cat was bowling along in fine style. I took the main off her completely as I did not want an uncontrolled gybe. She was romping along at 10 knots even with just the Genoa up. Mick turned into a "helm hog", and we had a fantastic sail until we closed with Cape St Vincent, where the wind gradually died off. We were by then on the port tack under full sail, moving slowly at about 4 knots. It had been a long night and I went below for some sleep after a Helen breakfast. I awoke some hours later to the sound of water rushing past. My eyes watered in the strong Sunlight, Mick and Helen were taking turns steering and the yacht was romping along at 10-11 knots, they were having a ball. Obviously that was what the big cat liked best, flat seas and about 15 knots of wind on the beam. In those conditions she was ideal. We slipped past the Algarve coast over a perfect day's sail and in the small hours of the morning closed with Huelau. We dropped anchor in a sheltered part of the estuary and waited for dawn.

Chapter 14

Early in the morning we upped anchor and motored to the waiting berth. I went in to find the Lagoon agents to get them to fit the pump. I was there when they opened. I identified myself and the yachts name. The lady fired up her computer; yes, she knew about us, no, a pump had not arrived. Instead they would send an engineer to fix the old one. I was not amused. We waited, the engineer arrived, when on board, then left for more hydraulic fluid, came back and announced "you need a new pump". Back at the agent's office a smiling Spanish man told me it was "no problem, we get you a pump tomorrow".

We could not stay on the waiting berth so I had to arrange a marina berth. The rates were really good, apparently it was a Government sponsored marina, so we only had to pay 33 euros per night, which was almost affordable. The berth I was allocated was the one closest to the harbour wall and cafés. I had to reverse the big cat all the way back, before swinging the yacht at just the right moment to get us in. It all went smoothly. A Scotch guy came and saw us, while we were having a coffee at the café. "nice bit of parking "he said, an opening gambit guaranteed to get a smile from me, I told him why we were there he said "welcome to the Hotel California" I said "what do you mean?" he said " it's like that Eagles line "you can checkout anytime you want but you can never leave", you will be here for ages, it's all this ""Manyana, manyana" business, we talked about other things but I was worried; we had already been on away from England for 9 days and we had a long trip still ahead. I simply could not afford to stay in harbour for long. We went shopping, Helen was enjoying herself, apart from the long uphill walk. When we came back it dawned on us that we had the swankiest yacht in the harbour - something that had never happened to me before. People were drinking their coffees, gazing with envy at it. So that night Helen lit up the little blue fairy lights that were stuck up the mast and all over the place, it looked good, but I did feel like a fraud!

The next day, the morning delivery time passed, so did the afternoons. "Tomorrow" said the Spanish bloke. The Scot across the marina was playing Eagles tracks, and I distinctly heard "Hotel California" blasting out. The morning after, the girl from the agents office was sent over "it's Saturday, your pump will not be delivered until Monday "I had to stop Helen from savaging her. I sent a message to my boss asking for advice, I received one back, "can you do the trip without it?" we had a hurried conference, the bottom line was if we did not go very soon, both my crew would run out of time and have to go home. There really was not much choice, if I wanted to get reimbursed for the money I had already laid out, we had to leave. We paid for our stay, I flipped the Spaniard a two fingered salute and we were off.

Chapter 15

I planned to stop at Gibraltar get more stores and fuel. Well when I say Gibraltar I mean a little Spanish marina just past it. It is 10 minutes' walk from the boarder but a lot cheaper. We had another good sail. Past Cape Trafalgar it became a bit too good and we rounded up into the wind and stowed the mainsail. As we came into the Gibraltar roads we attempted to roll away the foresail. It absolutely refused, so I attempted to drop it by un-clutching the halliard, the slug jammed, just like the last delivery a bolt had come out of the luff track. Unlike the last boat this was not some small blade foresail, this was a huge monster Genoa that was flapping around. It was either going to destroy itself or make the yacht so uncontrollable we would hit something. A solution had to be found. In the end I used an anchored tanker for a lee and sent Mick up the forestay in a Bosun's chair to unshackle the head of the sail from the slug. With that task accomplished we pulled the sail down and lashed it down to the foredeck. We rounded a little breakwater, it was blowing hard and I decided to anchor rather than risk an unknown marina in the dark.

Calling up Alcadesa marina in the morning was fairly futile, the person I spoke to could not speak English and my Spanish is not very good. The Westerly wind was still blowing a good 7 or more, so we went in and found an easy berth to tie up to. I walked over to the office and told them I needed a berth for a couple of days. They gave me one, although it was a horror story; down a tight row of yachts, with the Westerly wind fairly screeching behind us I would have to make a hard turn to starboard to get in, and miscalculating it would crunch us into a nasty concrete wall. I asked why we could not stay where we were, and was told we could if we paid extra. So

I went back to the cat and briefed Helen and Mick. I told them that when we made the turn it was not likely that we could keep on the windward side of the berth but we would drop onto the leeward side and rely on lots of fenders to prevent damage. Then after we had stopped we would put ropes onto the weather side and take the strain off. If there had been less wind I would have relied on the centre cleat but I did not want to take any chances of the cleat pulling out or any other kind of mishap. Also I asked Mick to walk over and wait at the berth we had been allocated with a big fender.

With just Helen on board we sprang out of our nice safe berth and left to get into what Helen thought was a certain disaster. In order to maintain control, I had to have speed, so we went down the row at a fair old clip, just before hitting the wall I gave the starboard engine full astern, she pivoted nicely into the berth, and at that point a tall South African from another cat arrived and started trying to get Helen to give him the Starboard head rope, I had to shout at him to make him go away in order to get the boat to land on the lee side square. If the head rope had been tight we would have swung around and bashed the port hand stern. Once sorted and moored fore and aft we took the strain off by putting ropes from the starboard side across to cleats and tightening them up. Then I had to go and find the South African and apologise for being rude.

Not long after a large mono hull yacht with a bowsprit came in, he had tried two other berths before the one just up wind from us, but he could not make the turn fast enough, he had one chance left, if he did not get into the last finger berth then he would piled up on the wall. As he came in, I caught the skipper's eye and got him to steer upwind of where he wanted to go and waved him to give it full power to get steerage way, then I was able to catch a breast rope from the bow and surge it on a cleat to brake him before he ploughed into the walkway. There was no doubt in my mind that they were really hard berths to get into with a brisk Westerly wind. But lovely and cheap!

We wandered over to Gibraltar; there were huge queues of road traffic to get in, but walkers had it easier and it was not long before we were treading across the main runway towards the city centre. Bizarre as it sounds the runway is part of the road, when a plane wants to land they shut it off! We had a look around and bought some familiar food, after which we had a few beers and went back. The wind was still howling and I decided we would wait before I tackled the forestay problem. The next day was the same, but in the afternoon I scaled the forestay and used Loctite to put the screws back in and checked them all. A lot were coming out, and I don't think the job was done right in the first place. I also had a good look at why the Genoa would not roll up. The angle at the top between the halyard and the slug was wrong - it was not steep enough, so when there was any strain on it, it would wrap the halyard around the top of the forestay and jam. I came to the conclusion that the sail was too small, so I extended the luff with some spectra cord. It then rolled away really easily.

I went over the weather forecast with my new South African friend, it looked like we would have strong Westerly's for the rest of the day. The next day it would drop down a bit, after that it would drop to nothing and then slowly over the next few days start to blow from the East. I pondered this, as I saw it we would not be wise to stay much longer, as if we lost the westerly wind we would have to motor, and if we stayed on the Spanish side of the Med we would only be able to stop in some very expensive marinas if the wind became too strong for us. Bearing in mind also that without an auto pilot we could only manage short watches, as well as adding a couple of hundred miles to the voyage, so we would become very exhausted really quickly. However, if we used the Westerly the next day and went down the Algerian coast, if it blew up we could duck in and anchor behind some handy bit of rock until it calmed down. It seemed like a good plan at the time. I was able to buy a full Gaz bottle off the South African. I must say it seemed bizarre to me that Gaz bottles were not easily available in Gibraltar.

Chapter 16

We left in the morning and at first we were in the lee of the land, but I resisted temptation and kept the mainsail stowed, once out into the straits I was glad I had. The next 15 hours were a hoot! The big cat was surfing on large waves and I got the record 17.1 knots! She handled it beautifully, with no threats of broaching and always under complete control. It was a shame when the wind gradually died off, but at least by then we were near Morocco, and had used hardly any fuel. The next day we were in Algerian waters. Lots of sword fish kept leaping out the water, something I had never seen before - very strange. Our yacht had an active AIS transponder on board. The Algerian coastguard called us up and wanted to know our intentions, and I explained we were on passage. Eventually they left us alone.

Days seem to melt into one but at least we had the scenery of the Algerian coastline to look at, and the odd fishing boat. I think Mick upset one on one of the nights, it was flashing its search light at us when I came up. Each day a new coast guard would call us up - it was not a problem, and I think some of it was just them practising their English. On the fourth day we were very tired, me and Mick were doing 2 hour watches, Helen was doing all the cooking and steering while we ate, and helping Mick on his watch. The big cat was so hard to steer most of the time Helen was not physically up to standing a full watch. The wind started to get up strong from the East, a dead noser, and we were not making much progress on our course so I decided to find a place to anchor. On the chart was a man-made harbour that promised a big breakwater that we could hide behind. We went towards it and the coast guard started calling us up. But I could not understand him. We arrived off the beach, in smooth water in the lee of the breakwater. It looked a good place to anchor and we dropped the hook, but it started to drag, so we pulled it up and tried again. This time it bit, but a small fishing dory came out of the harbour and the fisherman said we should go in. I said "no we are fine here" but he kept getting very close to our anchor warp with his outboard, and saying "come in." In the end I had decided to go in the harbour and have a look. So we hauled the anchor up and he offered to tow us, which I declined. The harbour looked very small, as we approached a RIB came out, full of men with AK47s - lots of them. I decided to go back to sea, and pointed that way to the men in the RIB, who I now saw were actually the local police, one of them shook his head and pointed to the harbour. Mick said "they got guns max", and I decided that their orders had to be obeyed - I did not think the owner of the Lagoon would be impressed with bullet holes in his boat.

As we entered the harbour following the RIB and the fishing boat, all the fishermen who were about, stopped and stared. The Lagoon is no doubt a yacht with a visual impact, and in this little scruffy harbour that was full of down at heel fishing boats, she might as well have been from a different planet. The harbour got smaller and smaller as we went deeper into it, finally we reached the end, there was another RIB already tied up to a pontoon. A man in a naval uniform indicated that we should moor there, so I span the cat around with its two diesels, one ahead and one astern, and backed into the space - that was too small. Mick and Helen had all the fenders out and we passed our ropes over. We had just got tied up and the Harbour Master told me to move it to another wall, the place he wanted me to go had an old tractor tyre hanging off a long rusty bolt. It looked like the yacht would get damaged there, so I refused. I think it was a long time since anyone had said "no" to this man, and he did not like it. But reluctantly let us stay where we were. Meanwhile the fisherman was doing something with one of our fenders, in fact he was attempting to steal it I think, because one of the policemen started beating him until he ran off. Ashore, when I looked there was also a lot of shouting - several men where filling up a hole with concrete, another man shouted at them, and they were working at the double, despite the heat. They were covered in grime sticking to the sweat, they did not look like they were doing it out of fun, it looked like a fatigue party. I began to feel a little uneasy.

The Harbour Master spoke English and asked to come on board, I answered "please do" he was accompanied by one of his men. I offered him coffee, which was declined. He asked why we had come into the harbour, I said "because of the wind". He nodded at that, then asked for my papers and everyone's passports. I produced them, "what is this?" he said when I gave him the copies of the registration and insurance. I said "copies, the originals were taken with the owner by mistake. "You are not the owner?" he asked "no, we are just delivering this yacht to Split" I told him. "I cannot accept these papers, they are not original, you must wait while I go and copy your passports" he said. With that he left. I had a sinking feeling that we might be there for a while. However he was soon back, and he returned our passports. His attitude had softened slightly; he accepted a cup of coffee and I showed him the paper charts with our route on and our destination, then he went through all the papers I had until he found a form I had filled in asking for permission to leave from the firm I was working for. "This is an original" he exclaimed in triumph! "This will do; I must make a copy. As he turned to leave he said, "This will be alright, but you have committed an infringement, you have no Algerian courtesy flag "I said, "I am sorry, I did not know we would be visiting your country, may we buy one?" He replied, "Do you have any money?" I said yes, euros and English pounds". His reply was "that is no good here, and there is no place to change it". Then he asked me if I needed anything, I said some fresh bread was all. He barked an order and the young policeman with him ran off, a few minutes later he reappeared with a black plastic bag full of fresh French sticks, and would not take any money for them. The harbour master then said "you will stay here until you have permission to leave, you have no visa so you must not get off the boat". He was perfectly civil, but not a man to cross. I saw him give an order to two soldiers who were in a small building nearby, he pointed to us, and I gathered we were now under an armed guard. Helen started cooking the dinner.

Chapter 17

Over the evening cars and disgorged men and boys came over to have a look at the yacht. The soldiers chased most away but two young men were allowed to come and talk to us. We invited them aboard and they took photos on their phones of each other, then left. Helen remarked that there were no women or girls to be seen. She was right - it was all very strange. Helen could not resist switching on the little blue fairy lights and lighting up the Lagoon like a Christmas tree. We had an early night, and we had a good night's sleep for a change.

We were awoken by the call to prayer, I got up and had a look around. The soldiers were still on watch, and all seemed fairly peaceful. A little later a man came and stared at us. He was in Muslim garb and just stood there, his expression was one of extreme hostility. I began to wonder if the soldiers were there to stop us getting off or stop others getting on. Whichever it was, I wanted to leave. I went over to the soldiers, gave them some cigarettes and asked if we could go (as the wind had gone down). The soldier understood and made a phone call. After a longish conversation, he said, "yes, you can go" as easy as that. I was so happy I forgot to look where I was going and near the yacht where the two pontoons were joined I did not notice a bigger than usual gap. My foot went through it and I scraped my leg as I fell. The soldier walked over, helped me up and asked if I was okay, obviously very concerned. I was fine, but limped back on board. There was still a lot of fishing boats moving around and I wanted to wait for them to stop before we left, as the harbour was very small. Thankfully they did stop and we let go the ropes and left the pontoon. A big crowd of fishermen were watching and Helen called

"Goodbye" and waved, the fishermen shouted things back, which I hoped were nice!

Algeria surprised me. Yes, you could say it was a bit of a culture shock, as I did not expect to see forced labour and brutality. On the other hand, we had entered their country without a visa, and proper paperwork. We had been treated with fairness by people who, once they knew us, were polite and helpful. I doubt if a yacht full of Algerians in the same circumstances would have received the same polite treatment from a British border agency officer.

Back at sea the East wind returned, but not quite as bad as the day before and towards the evening it died off, so we rolled away the genoa and motored with just the main up. I knew we would have to refuel at Tunisia. I had heard that fuel was a lot cheaper there. We still had 25% in the Port tank and nearly 50% in the starboard. And they are big tanks on the Lagoon, just about holding 1000 litres between them. The Yanmar 38 HP engines were all you could ask of a diesel, and they had so much power and the hulls were so easily driven, most of the time we only ever had one engine running at just 2000 revs to give us about 6-7 knots.

The dawn brought a fog, as it began to lift in the early morning sun we went past a small fishing dory. The occupants looked at us in astonishment. Then there was another one, and fairly soon we were dodging in and out of them. Mick came up to take his watch just as one small boat tried to come alongside. I started the other engine and gave both full ahead, the Lagoon jumped up to 9 knots and we dodged around the boat. The occupants shouted something, but I waved back and smiled and they did not chase. Up ahead I saw two more boats coming towards us, so we did the same trick and got past them as well. I saw what the fishermen were trying to sell us - Red Coral. I did not want it, and I did not want their beat up boats alongside either. One of them even waved a big knife at us. I told Mick to go and get the emergency steering bars, about the size of short scaffold bars they would make good clubs to repel boarders with if we had too. I wanted to go more offshore but as the visibility bettered we began to see the fleets of the boats went for miles outside us. At least as we were only about 3 miles off the coast, one of the many coast guard stations might see what was going on. And I think they did, because suddenly a fast patrol boat came up from astern, the small boats stopped trying to stop us. Until the patrol boat turned back, at which point the small boats started the game again. But then we came to the Tunisian border and we ran out of small boats.

This time I wanted no problems so I called up the Tunisian Coastguard and asked if it was okay to enter the port of Tabaka. The coastguard seemed puzzled, "what is your problem" he asked "no problem, I told him just checking if its okay for us to go there, I said. He didn't say of "course it is you dumb ass", but I think that's what he was thinking.

Tarbaka, is a stunning port to enter. The first thing you see is a big old castle on almost an island, then looking past it there is a Roman Amphitheatre. (It's actually a modern copy, still under construction, but it is a grand sight). There are two harbours, one is ancient and has not changed much in the last couple of thousand years. We wanted the more modern one. There was an empty stretch of wall, so we closed with it and moored up. A jeep with two policemen came racing towards us and I thought" here we go again". But they smiled made sure we were tied up properly and pointed to the Harbourmasters office before leaving. I asked Helen to stay with the yacht while I went and sorted out clearing in with Mick.

Chapter 18

At the Harbourmasters office we entered another world. The place was a bit rundown. None of the officials could speak English, so they had one of the dockside loafers who were hanging about outside come in. He could speak a little of my tongue, and I began to understand I had to pay 20 Dina for a stay of 2 days. That was OK, with the only exception being that I didn't actually have any Dina. A long conversation took place and it was agreed that the "interpreter" would escort us to our next stop - the police station, then customs, then to go and get some local currency, and finally I could pay them their 20 Dina.

So Mick and I walked with this guy (slowly, as it was hot) to the police station. Once there a long conversation took place between our man and the policeman on the desk. We would have to wait for the top man to arrive. The police station was equally as shabby as the harbourmasters office, and seemed to have once been painted by a visually impaired madman some years before. We all watched the TV, which was loosely screwed to the wall. Some time elapsed before a man in a shabby suit attempted to ride a moped through the door. This was the senior cop. Much conversation took place, followed by stamping of passports, and filling in of forms. Reeling from this surreal experience we were escorted on to the Customs office, by this time we also had a policeman in tow. At the Customs office our nerves were slightly soothed by the sight of a really pretty girl in a customs officer uniform manning the front desk. She called out to the back office when our interpreter informed her of our mission.

The top dog Customs office emerged from his office, he looked like he had just been woken and was still a bit sleepy and slightly annoyed. However not a man to shirk his duty he scratched an itch, reluctantly donning his uniform jacket over his vest (did I mention it was hot?) and entered into the protracted negotiations needed to resolve this clearly unusual problem of a yacht entering the port. The right forms were located except one; "Where is the manifest?" he thundered! It was the first time I have ever been asked for a manifest. In fact, I gathered that the Harbour Master was supposed to have given me a Manifest form to fill in. In the end, the big man (and he was big) reluctantly announced that he would "visit the yacht, and sort things out himself" - at least that was my understanding of the matter. I was a little worried as we had no Tunisian courtesy flag and no yellow Q flag up either. Our little party now consisted of me, Mick, our interpreter, the police man, and the chief Customs officer. The pretty girl stayed in the office to mind the shop. We sauntered over around the harbour, slowly to not raise a sweat (it was still very hot). The customs man had a penchant for bolloxing people on boats and he let loose a few good broadsides before we arrived at the Lagoon.

Things became a tad weirder with the sight that greeted us back at the yacht. There was a small crowd of women dressed in full burkas photographing each other with their mobiles on the bows of the Lagoon, our still not "cleared in" yacht. Several others appeared from inside as we boarded. One was still staring and exclaiming at the galley with its dish washer and microwave as we entered. The custom man and the policeman all pretended they had not seen anything and the crowd quickly dispersed, Helen said "Hi, you have been gone ages. The locals like the boat". I asked her to make some coffee, and she set to. The custom man wanted a tour, to which I was happy to oblige. He wanted to know which cabin was which, and he also asked "who does she belong to" and pointed at Helen, who gave him the dangerous slitty eyed look that usually proceeds physical violence. I said brightly "she is with me ". I got a grunt in exchange for this information. He asked if we had any cigarettes on board, all the tobacco on board was produced - Mick and Helen had bought lots in Gibraltar. All the pouches were laid out and he picked one at random and opened it and had a good sniff. It passed whatever test it was under and we got onto the subject of alcohol. We did not have any of that, but it took quite a bit of demonstrating that we did not in actual fact have any booze on board. Once persuaded we all sat drinking coffee, a tad exhausted. The custom man worked up to a delicate problem "you have to pay some money" he said, I answered "okay, to you?" "No not to me, pay that man" he said pointing to the policeman, "and what should I pay him? "I asked, "What you think" was the enigmatic answer. "10 euros?" I offered "yes that is fine", he smiled a broad smile.

Now he was in a happy mood we all ambled back to his office, where I spoilt everything by admitting I could not pay the official charge for the form of 1 Dina because I did not have any. He sent me off to the "International Hotel" to get some money changed. I did so (which was a little protracted) and made my way back to the customs office sometime later. The girl was there, I had discovered how little 1 Dina was, and in a moment of insanity offered a five Dina note to cover the charge and the trouble. The girl looked distraught and shouted out to the customs man, who once more emerged from his den sans uniform jacket. In a bad mood again he demanded 1 Dina. I found a coin and took back the note, he smiled, donned his jacket and hat, took a postage stamp, stuck it (after a good lick) onto a form, stamped the whole lot and said in English "welcome to Tunisia". I wobbled back to the yacht. On the way I paid the Harbourmaster his 20 Dina and gave 5 Dina to our "interpreter", I also broached the subject of fuel. He smiled when he understood what was needed and went off to arrange it.

Back at the yacht, the crew wanted shore leave, and so did I. The good port of Tabarker was so totally alien to anything we had ever seen before it just begged for a good exploring. We had to wait for the man to come back with the news about fuel, but he was not long and said "tomorrow" "how much?" I asked," 1 Dina a litre" he said, I forgot to look shocked, and stupidly agreed, indeed to me that was a good price, about half of what I would have paid in Gib and about a third of the asking price in most of the U.K.'s marinas! I wonder what I could have gotten it down to.

We locked up the boat and went exploring, enjoying a fine lunch during which Mick was asked if he was American by some kids. Then we went to the Amphitheatre and tried out the acoustics. It is clever how someone on the stage can be heard from a long way away. On the way up we were amused by a local con man attempting to trick some money out of us, he pretended to find a £2 coin on the pavement, then he gave it to Helen and said "it's no good to me, you have it" she said "thanks, here is a Dina or two" - next minute he had his fingers in Helen's purse, Mick and I growled at him and I think he realised we were not stupid tourists and he legged it sharpish. That was the only unpleasant thing that happened, and we continued to wander around, taking in the sights. There was a good mix of different styles, girls dressed in hot European fashion mixed with ladies in burkas, everyone seemed to get along. The only exception was an army outpost that was strangely covered in razor wire, complete with hard-eyed alert sentries posted at every corner.

Later that day we enjoyed a good meal and Mick went off to find a beer or two. I did not want to join him - call me old fashioned but I think in a Muslim country it is showing respect not to go on a bar crawl. Mick and I did not see eye to eye on this and he had a thirst that needed quenching. It must have been maybe more than two, because he did not make it back until the very small hours. I was worried for him, but he arrived back on aboard talking nonsense and we all got some shut eye.

I do love waking up in a strange land, especially if it is warm and sunny. At first light I was bustling around annoying both Helen, who is not a morning person, and Mick who was unwell. Having hacked everyone off, we went shopping. Helen and I proceeded to have a row. I don't even remember what it was about, and we went in different directions. Soon we met up again, and had some chocolate croissants, then once all that was over we reluctantly left our nice harbour berth and went to get fuelled up. That was not much of a problem; we took 440 litres and just about filled the tanks. Then I went over to the customs to make sure we could leave. He sent me to the police station. I waited there for an hour or so, 30 minutes of which 3 police men spent attempting to get a good image off their stamp that had run out of ink. Having successfully stamped our forms I then went to customs The pretty girl called him from the back room, he emerged, saw who it was and putting his jacket on called to a couple of his buddies to come and see the yacht, and we all trooped out to the fuel berth. A long conversation ensured, and another search of the yacht, coffee was made and when it was discovered that we had not spent all the money we had changed, Helen and Mick were dispatched back to the Hotel to convert it back into Euros, as no Dinas must leave the country!

While they were gone I made small talk - very small talk as my French is rubbish. One of the customs men insisted I should give him whiskey, but settled for the very last can of larger the Russian's had left behind. After a while the lead Customs man said he really must be going and I went with him for my papers decorated with the postage stamp.

Helen and Mick had returned, but had been unable to convert any money, so we left anyway and later clever Helen was able to sell it on E Bay, retrieving her money that way. I think we were all sorry to go as we did not have enough time there and I would love to revisit the place soon - quirky but full of character would be how I sum Tunisia up.

Chapter 19

Back at sea after too short a time everyone was a bit grumpy. I had kept from them a horrible fact - that was our last stop and we still had about 800 miles to go. Mick and Helen had run out of time, I had run out of money. Not to mention that it would be very foolish to stop at an Italian port because I had heard that those guys were red hot on correct paper work and would even want to see an Italian translation of our insurance documents. No, the only way I could see of salvaging anything out of the trip would be to do this leg with no more stops. I broke the news to the crew, they were not too happy.

Morale continued its decent later that night. We were crossing the Sardina channel and I wanted to keep plenty of sail up, not only on account of the greater speed but also stability. The crew wanted no sail and just engine. I explained that our active AIS was transmitting and although there were many ships, we were not going to cross any shipping separation lanes, so technically we were the stand on vessel always if we were under sail if we only met ordinary ships. I would not have pushed my luck, but with the AIS transmitting our position, and what kind of vessel we were, I felt fairly safe. One of the other ships even warned another tanker about us, very reassuring. Mick came to take over the watch. When I later came back to relive him I could not help but notice that the steering position was covered in tobacco and fag ash. Mick smoked like a chimney when he was stressed, so I asked him if the watch was a bit busy. F****** ships all over the place, he answered. There was a nasty cross sea, and the Lagoon was a nightmare to keep on course, so I was very glad when the sky gradually lightened. Another day brought us into Italian waters, first signified by a police helicopter that almost landed on our stern while it tried to read the name and see our national flag. Night brought more weirdness, and a patrol boat lit us up at one point with its searchlight, but that was all.

During the next day things settled down and I expected that since we had our AIS going the Italian coastguard would have figured that we were not up to anything naughty. However, the next night when I had gone off watch and was deep in the land of nod, I was woken by a shout from Helen. Belting up in my boxers I was just in time to greet a blacked out patrol boat as it came alongside. I took the lines and put out fenders, then went and got the required passports. I was expecting difficulty, but as the captain was examining the passports one of his crew went rigid, much like a pointer hunter dog. In the silence that followed we could plainly here a high performance motor boat going like a bat out of hell from the direction of Albania. Much shouting of "pronto" and such like ensued, and I chucked off the ropes, managing to grab our passports just before the boat went hard astern to chase the blacked out vessel.

A school of dolphins showed up the next night. Much smaller than their Atlantic cousins, they made up for this by dint of their amazing aquatic prowess. The wind went around to the West and we sailed without the engine for some days. And then finally we were almost there.

The Croatians have a strange clearing in procedure; you must go to the nearest customs station and pay for a cruising licence. The problem started when I called up the Croatian coastguard. I was directed to an Island that was a good deal out of our way. Then the owner rang up. I took the call he asked me where we were. I told him and he suggested that we clear in at a different island Kuracula. He was pleased we had made it despite no auto pilot, and suggested that we keep the yacht for ourselves for a few days. This was very kind of him, but contrary to the data I had been getting from my boss, who said we were late. So we went there and found the marina which was about the size of a swimming pool. The wind was up, we came in and I put us alongside another yacht as we picked up the lines to pull us off the dock. It was then that we found out that we had to go to the customs dock instead until we had cleared in. Cursing, we extracted ourselves without damaging anything and found the Customs dock. A customs man was very unimpressed by our attempt at a Croatian flag, as I had just hoisted the French flag up sideways. We did not have a "Q" flag either and he got well out of his pram at that too. We were escorted to his office where I was given the bill, but Helen was good enough to lend me the money after I rang the agent in Split and he confirmed he would reimburse me with cash as soon as we got to Split. We went off to a cash machine and got the money out. Bill paid and we wandered around for a bit. It was a very beautiful town, and very hot. I wanted a coffee, but the custom man found us and told us we were not allowed to stay in the customs berth, not even for a coffee. So we left.

It became clear that we would not get to Split before nightfall. I called up the agent and he suggested we anchor up someplace, as there was work being done in the harbour. However, Mick was champing at the bit to get off the yacht and have a beer. So I continued. We found the harbour and worked our way in past the construction and soon were tied up. It was very good to have arrived but it was late and all the bars were shut.

Chapter 20

In the morning I was able to get some sugar for Helen (we had run out) that made her sweeter, and then we started cleaning up. Then things went bad. The agent came aboard, surly and snotty. He was abrupt and told us to clean up the boat so we could get through the inspection and then transfer to another yacht because the one we had brought in was supposed to be going out on charter. I had to stop Helen from smacking him one. We knew he was lying - the owner himself had told us to take the rest of the week off. There was no "well done you made it", even though we had no Auto Pilot. When we had cleaned up his two stooges came on board and the humiliation continued. They were making a big thing out of the small tear in the sail I had repaired saying that the sail had to be taken off and taken to the sail makers. I said, "Well, the repair has done us the best part of 2 thousand miles, why don't you leave it in until the winter when the sail goes for a service?" No, that was not good enough; it had to be repaired "properly". Then they made a list of all the cracks that had appeared in the deck like it was our fault. They did not seem surprised when I showed them how the ropes were all dropping to bits and stopping us from reefing. When one of them started to give me grief about rust stains in the bottom of the gaz bottle locker I ordered them to get off the boat before I threw them off. I told them to get their boss over I had had enough of them.

The agent came over and started going over the yacht. When we got to the foredeck he saw the lashing I had put on the foresail to extend the tack so we could roll it away, "what is this" he snarled. "It's the only way the sail works, it's too short," I told him, we had to unfurl the sail so he could see and he had to admit that the sail was too small and from another yacht. This was his fault because he had done the original checks when the yacht had left the yard in France. Then I told him about the anchor, he said, "come to my office in 1 hour".

An hour later I walked in, "you have not told your boss about the anchor problem?" "no "I said, "then you pay me for it and I will not tell him" "he said. "I don't see why I should. It was not our fault we lost it, the chain was too short" I told him. His reply was "No there was 85 meters of 12mm chain on it, you owe us 1400 euros." I told him to get lost and walked out.

My phone rang not long after. It was N.. my boss. He was not happy; "What happened?" I told him and he was surprisingly calm; "you do not talk to the owner; I will sort this out" he said. Mick went ashore for a drink. I went to the chart plotter. I could (as it had the tracker enabled) prove that when we had anchored behind Finesterre our scope was 160 meters, which is the length of the nylon rode, plus 20 meters (the chain that was there). I took photographs of the screen, and I even tried to show the agent, but he was not interested. We stayed there another day while Mick was attempting to drink Split dry, and I rang and asked my Boss to book him a flight for the next day, which he did. I had trouble waking him at 05.00 to catch the bus, but we just made it. Helen and I went for a walk around Split, which is stunningly beautiful. There are ancient parts of it that are Roman and have not changed in thousands of years. Back in the marina I took Helen for a meal and we were pleased at the food, wine and how inexpensive it was. The only fly in the ointment was the agent, who was now refusing to return the forms I had filled in and he was meant to sign off. Helen had a good idea: she suggested I tell him we were staying so that we could meet up with the owner on Friday. So that is what I did. The forms magically materialised and the agent told me I was off the hook as my boss had agreed to pay on his insurance. He also warned me not to talk to the owner again. So once out of earshot I phoned up the owner and told him I had been ordered not to talk to him, but that everything that had happened was in his log book, which was his property and was in his chart table. Then I called my boss, explained my credit card was maxed out and asked him to book flights, this he did. The next morning Helen and I left and made our way home.

I was not really surprised when I had an email telling me 1400 euros for the anchor had been deducted from my fee. I made some enquires and apparently if I wanted to sue I might have been able to make a case; after all no-one had verified that there was 85 meters of chain on the anchor. However, I had to admit I had made a mistake. The fact that even without the Auto pilot, the wrong foresail, a small crew and no papers we had managed to get that yacht undamaged to its destination did not seem to carry any weight with my boss but the owner was pleased. He called me up after he had read the log and told me to forget about the sail problem, "it happens" he said. I asked him about the anchor and he said a new one had been put aboard, "what about the one I bought?" "It is not here" he said after he had looked, then he went to see the agent and got him to give it back. Later he emailed me and asked how much it had cost. After I told him he transferred money into my account to cover it, and a little more.

Apart from that little brightness the whole show had been a financial disaster in a month I had made £194 profit, for that I had worked 18 hours a day at least seven days a week for four whole weeks! In hindsight I should never have gotten involved with this big delivery company as I simply did not have the money behind me to finance my involvement. Once I had signed the contract in the

U.K. half of my fee was deposited in my bank account, then when I arrived with my crew and found things were not as they should have been I was boxed in. I simply did not have the funds to hang about and sort the yacht out. Also if I had not have delivered the catamaran I would have been libel at that point for the full cost of any delivery that took place because I could not fulfil my contract. I think this is what my father fondly calls "the thorny path to wisdom!"

Chapter 21

After that financial flop, I needed to raise some money quickly, so I called an old mate who was in charge of Greater London Hire couriers (city branch) and asked if I could work as a cycle courier. He was pleased to see me. I had mentioned him in my last book, so I gave him a copy, we talked over old times and Steve (Purkiss) gave me a uniform and various bits of kit, wishing me luck. I embarked on my first day back in the saddle. The weather was nice and sunny. Strangely after the stress of the last month the London City traffic seemed to me to be almost tranquil - all I had to do was wobble about picking up and delivering letters. The pay was not wonderful, and the hours (because I had to catch the train back Basildon after 19.45) were a bit long. But I did enjoy it. It did not last, however. An old mate I had not seen for 15 years, (Dave the squaddie) called me up. "What are you doing?" he asked. "Push bike courier" I answered. When he stopped laughing he said "You still have a class 2 truck licence?" "Yes" Well get your ass over to C and S recovery, they are covering the Olympics, and need drivers to sit around 18 hours a day at £10 per hour." "Right o." I made my apologies to Steve, but he was fine about it. I got up to C and S but I was just a little too late as all the cushy jobs had gone. Since I had a class 2 licence I was told they would train me to be a recovery driver, and I was put with another guy out on the road to learn the ropes. I think I should draw a veil over the next two weeks. In my defence I can only say that although I have the licence I had not driven anything for almost three years, and the loony that "trained" me had a wicked sense of humour. When I found out that there was no insurance and if I damaged anything I was expected to pay for it, (drop even a clip on a range rover and that's a few grand!) my enthusiasm ebbed away for the job. The other pain was I had to take a truck home each night and there just was not space to park it. I was quite glad when I was told I had not made the grade and they could not give me a job.

I received a timely phone call from my good buddy Chris Lewis who was running a small ferry boat in the river Medina on the Isle of Wight. He asked me to help him as crew over the next Isle of Wight festival that was happening at the end of the week. He warned me that the hours would be long, but it sounded like fun so I told him to count me in.

Nothing is ever simple. It rained, the campsite and the festival became a quagmire, cars struggled to get in and huge traffic jams ensured. The only mode of transport that was not hampered was of course water traffic! However, Chris had a problem. Instead of sharing an abundance of passengers, a business competitor had taken the opportunity to pull a fast one and damage Chris's one chance of making a killing that year. The crafty sod had done a deal with the big ferry company that brought the passengers to the Island - they paid one fee for a ticket and that entitled them to small ferry rides to and from the festival, and Chris was not cut in.

The first day was horrible, I was stationed near the ferry terminal's gate to sing out "ferry trips to the festival". Lots of people came up but all had tickets and I had to direct them to the large queue that was growing at one end of the pier. The taxi drivers complained that I was stealing their fares, and I had to move further away, but I was allowed a sign! The crowd began to get hostile as they could see boats coming in, filling up and going away while our boat stood by with just a few people on it. After half an hour we left. Chris was upset; he was up against a large fleet of boats this guy had brought in, but as Chris was the main ferry for the Island Marina that owned the access pontoon that everyone who was going to the Festival had to use, he had been given the opportunity to have total control, but had allowed the other guy in because Chris just did not have enough boats to handle the crowds.

As I tried to keep Chris's spirits up several thoughts had struck me. First of all, the Festival was over several days, and it was raining. When those many thousands of people wanted to leave they would be impatient. Another thing was that the landing place was very shallow at low water and some of the boats we were up against would have difficulty getting in, and Chris knew the way in and out better than anybody. He told me he could get in at any state of tide. Something else to bear in mind was the economics. Chris had a diesel driven heavy old motor boat called Lew Maru, the engine a 40hp Iveco had been fitted with a Hydrogen cell made by Hydroxy. Chris was running it to see if it did work, because he wanted the franchise in the area if it did. From what I had seen it worked very well, cutting the expected fuel use down to 2.8 litres an hour from what I would have expected to be about 4 -5 litres per hour. Some of the other boats were using petrol outboards, so in well loaded boats they were going to be very expensive to run.

I told Chris that all we have to do was carry as many people as possible for the first couple of days and it will sort itself out after that. And that's what we did; we made a point of being the first boat to start running, and the last boat to stop, Chris's girl Cath was running a pub were I stayed while working but I did not see much of my bed. We were finishing at 02.00 in the morning some times, and we were not making fortunes, but the payback was coming.

The second night while I was on the landing place at the festival, a RIB came in with Edmund Whelan my good friend on board. His party included Amber and her friend Peter. As Edmund was there I gave him a brief outline of the fuel-saving equipment on board our ferry boat. He was very interested and said he would ring me in a few days about it, and then he and his pals went off to the VIP tent while Chris and I went to find some more passengers.

People started having enough of the mud and leaving after a couple of days. On the second day of the retreat (well that's what it looked like) Mr clever clogs (our competitor) could not keep up with the crowds. Time after time we would arrive, moor next to the gangway and be looked at by crowds of people who wanted to go home for baths, warm food and soft beds. But we had briefed the security guards that we could only accept cash-paying people. Some stumped up the fare anyway just to get off. I collected their unused return tickets as well. The management of the marina became very unhappy with Mr Clever Clogs because this situation was making people very cross. But the straw that broke the camel's back came in the afternoon at low water. Mr Clever Clog's biggest boat had to lay off and ferry people out in small boats. Although we needed just as much water as them, Chris knew the channel. Mr Clever Clogs stood on the end of the pontoon and shouted at Chris not to come alongside in case we blocked the channel, but we did! Our keel did clip the sand slightly, but it did not even slow us and we arrived at our spot and started taking on a full load. Mr Clever Clogs then waved in his bigger boat that needed the same amount of water as we did, which promptly ran aground a short distance from the pontoon. Luckily it was not quite in the channel and we were able to get past. As we departed I told Chris to radio him and get a deal. It worked. Mr Clever Clogs agreed to give Chris almost the same as a full fair for every ticket he collected and gave him. He didn't know about the one's I had been stashing!

We had a lot of fun, even if we had worked long hours, but I was very interested in the hydrogen cell. I met with the local agent (Clive Smith) and talked to him about it. As it happened the next week the developer (John Gout from Holland) would be over the next week. I wanted to see if I could get a franchise as well, and see what Edmund Thought about it too. He said perhaps we could all meet up next week on Chris's ferry. I left it like that and went home.

Chapter 22

I brought Helen down with me the next week and we stayed on Chris's yacht in the Island Marina. On the Saturday we met up with Clive and I met John. Chris took us in his ferry to West Cowes where Edmund appeared in his RIB. While Helen went shopping we got down to business. It was great watching Edmund work. He extracted all the important information rapidly in a no-nonsense manner, as all the equipment was there and he could see it working. It was simple - a small amount of electricity was taken from the alternator when the engine was running, and this then led to a cathode and an anode that was in an electrolyte solution. The Hydrogen came out of the bottle the solutions was kept in and was fed into the engine's air inlet manifold. There was a fan to keep the whole thing cool as well. It was possible to buy similar equipment on the internet. However, this set up was CEU approved; something no-one else has apparently.

Sadly, I had been misled - the franchises were not up for grabs. Instead John and Clive would be training people to install the units for a fixed price, and then do the servicing. Edmund did the number crunching and in a phone call later that day said he would happily do any legal work they needed, but the price of the unit and the servicing was more than the fuel it would save a small yacht over the years, so he could not see how it would take off. He had a point; really it needed a big manufacturer of engines to pick up the idea. It's not new technology - it has been around since about 1908! All the small amount of Hydrogen does is allow the diesel to burn hotter and quicker, and so boost power and efficiency. Up to 40%! In fact, this one piece of technology could go a long way in handling the fuel problems that face the world. If all the people who run internal combustion engines suddenly used 40% less fuel the hyena's who profit from this blatant waste of scarce resources would take a hit. So maybe that is why it's ignored by the big boys.

Obviously I was not going to make much money out of this venture if I became involved. Fortunately, a few small yacht delivery jobs came up. The first was from Richard who asked if I would do the sea trials on his trimaran "Trinity". Since my last experience with this 45-foot monster she had been worked on for almost three years, many thousands had been spent and I was very interested to find out what she was like. The last time we had met she had distinguished herself by becoming the only boat I had not been able to deliver to the requested destination, for reasons that will become apparent.

Chapter 23

About three years before in November I had a message from Richard Ayres, a yacht surveyor I had done some work for in the past. He asked me if I would deliver a 14 metre Trimaran from Southampton to St Katherine's marina in London. I said I would and he passed on the details of the owner. The Owner, also called Richard sent me some photos, and as they looked okay I agreed that I and Helen would meet him and some others down at the river Itchen to first of all check her out and then assist with the delivery.

The forecast was for North Easterly winds, it was going to be cold but I reasoned that the hard bit would be from Beachy Head to Ramsgate, once past that part we should have had a good sail. Helen and I arrived at the Marina and I told the security guard in the office what we were there for, the man had a good laugh, and said the last delivery crew ran away and vowed never to set foot on her again. This is not the kind of thing you want to hear as a delivery skipper. We went aboard anyway and started making ourselves familiar with the vessel. She was unlike anything I had sailed before, being 45-foot long and 27 foot wide. She had two 9 horse outboards to provide power. I had to free up the gear change controls to get them to engage gears. But once that was done they started up and ran smooth enough. While I was checking the sails, there was a message from the owner to get the biggest genoa ready because we would need it, I found this big baby in a locker and humped it to the forestay ready for hoisting.

I put some reefs in the main, that was easy enough, and then I pulled out the staysail. All of that worked fine. I took Helen off to buy some grub and when we arrived back I worked out a good passage plan - we needed to leave about 18.00 to catch all the tides. But by 19.00 we were still waiting for the owner and crew, and when the three of them finally showed up we cast off. Richard had brought Mark who worked with him. Mark had sailed before, but his pretty girlfriend had not. The first obstruction to a successful delivery reared up some minutes later. Although I had worked out that we could fit under the bridge, it did not look like it. We did, however, and just for a second I thought it was going to be an easy trip, ha-ha! Not long after this Helen asked for hot water to be piped to the forward heads.

Richard went into the engine room to turn the appropriate tap, a short while later he came and saw me and said "a pipe has come off, the 200 gallons that was in the tank are now in the middle bow section's bilge". "Okay, you had best pump it out then" I told him, "there is no bilge pump up there" he said, "you and mark had better get busy with a bucket then". I said. While they set about that Helen steered and I set the main and the staysail. Then I dragged the monster genoa back to the cockpit because the wind was on the nose and we would not need it until we got into the Thames Estuary. I then hanked on the working jib. This whole procedure took ages, but at last we had a wind just forward of the beam and I could hoist the stay sail and jib and stop the engines. By then the bucket team had also finished their mission and the bow section was dry.

It was bitterly cold and various people started going down with sea sickness as we got into the open sea. I was heading for the Looe Channel and I saw the starboard Green flash I wanted but we were making large amounts of leeway and I had to start an engine to miss it, even then we got so close that I thought I might of clipped it, Richard the owner thought we had, because the light lit up his cabin. Trinity now started to romp, we were hitting about 11 knots, and I hoped all our troubles were behind us. How wrong could I be?

The genny stopped working not long after we passed Brighton. As the whole of the galley was powered by electric that meant the end of hot meals and tea. As if this was not bad enough the port engine refused to start when I tried it. As the wind came more onto the nose I started the starboard engine, it ran very spasmodically. I was working with Richard to attempt to restart the genny, but no matter what I did it would not fire up. I asked him to shut down everything not absolutely necessary for navigation at night. Sadly, we had to have the two chart plotters on as there was no way of isolating them. At this point the starboard engine joined his mate and went on strike. Trinity chose her moment to reveal her dark side, as we hardened up to attempt to give Beachy Head a good clearance she came up into the wind, stopped and started to go backwards, building up to 6 knots, and nothing I did with the wheel had any effect! After about 500 meters she fell back onto her original tack and carried on.

As we neared the shipping lane further into the channel, I attempted to tack. The going astern at 6 knots thing was repeated, in the end we had to "wear ship" to get her on the starboard tack. To add to our freezing early morning nightmare, the tide had set against us, and the amount of lee way we wear making became glaringly obvious. Trinity had very little in the way of draught, about 1 meter, and a lumpy sea was running, combined with the headwind and the foul tide, she was hardly making any true miles towards her destination. I began to think we would be foolish to carry on. The extreme cold, lack of sleep, sea sickness and no hot food or drink had sucked the energy out of most of the crew, I could not but worry about how we would handle attempting the

Thames estuary in the coming night. Bearing in mind that we could well have run out of battery charge by then. A haven was needed, but where?

Chapter 24

I looked in the Reeds and got the phone number for Newhaven marina. But I was informed that we were too wide. So I tried Sovereign marina in Eastbourne – surprisingly, we would just fit through their lock gates. I explained that both our engines were down and we were struggling to make over the tide. I was told by the helpful staff that they would have their launch standing by to help when we did get near.

It took us three hours to cover the last few miles into the marina, and then only because Richard had managed to get the starboard outboard working at low revs. All hands grabbed fenders and we squeezed into the lock. The launch helped us out of the lock, and then we tied up alongside a long empty pontoon. Helen and I stayed behind to clean up while Richard and his friends dashed back to London. It had been a very strange delivery trip, and horribly expensive for Richard. I was thoroughly confused about Trinity - on the one hand she had masses of space below and a saloon to die for, off the wind she was incredibly quick, she had good directional stability, and felt very good to sail. On the other hand, she made an astonishing amount of leeway without the help of the engines. Tacking without engines was also as much fun as Russian roulette. I told Richard I would be prepared to carry on with the delivery, but only if the outboards and the genny were fixed.

Six months later I received a call from Richard asking me to come down to Sovereign marina and help him take Trinity back to Southampton so Helen and I went down there. The outboards ran, but the generator was still dead, however the batteries were fully charged and he had bought a new "suitcase" type genny as a back-up. When we tried it, it refused to start. It had been running earlier that day. Still, Southampton was only about twelve hours away so we should not really have a problem. So I agreed to leave with the next fair tide, at 18.00 hrs if I remember correctly. We managed to get through the lock gates (two sets) without problems, and made it to the open sea. Then the port engine stopped. The wind was very light and from the West, I had the main up and the working sails but we still needed a bit of help from the Starboard engine, so I was less than happy when the Starboard engine quit too. Richard had been trying to get the port one going, but he immediately turned his attention to the Starboard one. Helen and I sailed the boat, trying all manner of different sail combinations but no matter what I could not get Trinity to tack cleanly and the leeway was just too excessive to live with. A couple of times she did her party trick of sailing backwards out of control so at 0200 I said "enough is enough we are going back". We arrived with a spluttering starboard motor at 06.00 and as we waited in the lock I attempted to get some sleep. I had hardly got my head down when a man came on board and asked to look at the engines. He immediately found the problem, the fuel bulbs were on back to front! The arrows were pointing the wrong way, so that was why the engines were starving of fuel.

Helen had run out of time and sense of humour so she caught the train back home. I desperately wanted some sleep but agreed to carry on with Richard later that day at 19.00. The forecast was for no wind at all that night. I did get a bit of shut eye and the flags were hanging straight down as we locked out again, with only one person available to get a fender in if I got it wrong I was a tad anxious as we squeezed past the unforgiving concrete of the locks, but we made it with no problems - surprising really because Trinity would not steer with the rudders until she was doing about 3 knots, so I could only use the engines, and the starboard one had a slight delay before it would go into gear...

We had a dream of a trip, apart from the lack of tea, the diesel cooker not working and we did not have enough electric to spare to use the electric kettle. What we lacked in hot beverage we made up for with a flat sea and an easily driven hull, a sky full of stars and a fair tide. We were coming up the river Itchen the next morning, against the tide, in the torrential rain that had started to fall. I called up the mariner office at Shamrock mariner and asked him what berth we should go into. He gave me a number, I went past and thought "surely not" it was really difficult to get into but I span Trinity around and squeezed in somehow. We were just getting the ropes sorted when the radio came to life and the man said "not that one, go on the hammerhead". Very miffed I got her out and lined up for the hammerhead, the problem was that the tide was ebbing hard and it would be broadside to us pushing hard on the starboard hull and forcing us onto the pontoon. To make matters worse a big shiny motor yacht was moored ahead across our path, if I gave it too much power we would ram our stainless steel bow roller right through it. I came in and stopped her about 2 meters off, and she came in sweet as you like, but just when I though all was well, Trinity started to turn to starboard, I needed to give a little squirt of forward on the starboard engine, but I just knew if I did we would hit the yacht in front, so I left the helm and attempted to get a fender in place to take the bump, too late, we gave the pontoon a very slight knock.

Richard was not happy. He studied the damage closely - a bit of paint about the size of a fifty pence piece was scuffed. We had words, I could not understand what he was so upset about. He then said "don't you know how much this paint job cost?" I said "I have no idea - £4000?" his reply shocked me "closer to £23,000!" I could see then why he was upset, but those four transits of the double lock gates at Eastbourne where one small screw up would have done far more damage flashed before my eyes. I was glad the trip was over. We had a calmer talk in the saloon. I told him I thought that Trinity needed dagger boards and bigger rudders to make her sail better. He told me he was not happy with the outboards and would be replacing them with electric drives and putting two new generators in to power them. He paid me, winching at the bill which was very high for such a short trip, but he had to pay for me and Helen's travel, two days of my time one of Helen's and my travel back. We rode back on the same train to London where we shook hands for what I thought was the last time and said goodbye.

Chapter 25

Three years down the line and Richard sent me an email asking if I was available to take Trinity for sea trials. All that time she had been in boatyards having major work done on her, so I was intrigued to find out what the differences the changes had made so a date was agreed, and as well as Helen Richard wanted me to bring someone else. I could think of no-one better than my old sailing buddy Peter Stower.

Peter drove us down, and we picked up Richard from Southampton airport train station. With all the driving about we did not actually arrive at Hamble point marina and board Trinity until 10.00hrs. Helen was dispatched with Peter to get some food. I started going over the changes that had been made. Just then the rest of the crew arrived. Mark and Mo Young, who had sailed with us on the Southampton to Eastbourne debacle, were once more giving it a whirl and they had brought Mark's mother and her man friend so there would be 8 of us.

The new dagger boards suited Trinity; they stuck up in the air at angled slightly outwards. Mark and I hauled the downhaul lines and they were deployed and cleated off. The next job was to put the rudder blades into their carbon fibre housing. The rudder blades like the dagger boards were stunning to behold, and made also of carbon fibre. They fitted nicely into the housings and were kept down by nylon straps.

The next operation was to lower the electric drive pods into the water, which took a bit of doing because the pins that had to be pulled out had corroded, but after they had been released each drive slid down its tracks until it was immersed. Then Richard announced that we needed fuel, so our first task was to leave the pontoon, negotiate the Hamble mid-river moorings, get into the main channel then somehow get past all the Sunday morning traffic and go up river to the fuel pontoon. Straight away I realised there was a problem. The electric drives were silent at low revs, and the props did not give the trust I was expecting, so at first I thought they had not kicked in, but then if I gave too much power so I could hear them Trinity started turning too fast, and it took a few buttock-clenching minutes before I got the hang of it. When we arrived at the fuel berth there was a queue, so we had to stay on station, not blocking the fairway and ready to pounce as soon as there was space. I did not believe the batteries would have enough charge in them to support all the driving we were doing so we kept the generators going. After about half an hour of this performance a space became available and we charged in. It was at this point that I discovered that Trinity did not like stopping quickly, with the starboard drive going at full astern she seemed to take ages to slow down and stop. We got a stern spring to the fuel man and motored against it to bring us alongside. Then at last we could start taking on fuel. Finally, with a full tank we could leave.

By then it was almost mid-day. I did a quick work out of the tide - we had a couple of hours of ebb left and the wind was a light W.S.W. so we could reach into Osborne bay, turn around and reach back again. If there were any problems at least we would not be having to contend with a foul tide.

While we were still in the Hamble River Helen asked for the hot water to be switched on for the galley sink. Richard obliged and the pipe duly blew off, flooding the galley. "Here we go again" I thought, then outside we attempted to hoist the brand new main, and we discovered that the halliard was wrapped around the top mast step. Richard had a bosun's chair and I was soon hoisted up to the mast head to free the rope.

Once we had fitted the top batten to the sail we proceeded to hoist the mainsail. It was very hard work with far too much friction, but at least it was up. We pulled out the stay sail and Trinity began to move sweetly, after which we hauled up the electric drive pods. The next job was to pull out the genoa. Once sheeted in Trinity began to romp, up to 10 knots as easy as pie, but were was Richard? I found him below, disconnecting the chart plotter so he could swap it with the one on the steering station. I showed him how we were doing; he was mildly pleased and went back to his electrics. I looked at my watch and could see that the tide would soon be on the turn. I decided we would broad reach into Osbourne bay, then tack round and close haul back to the Hamble. That way if we had any problems the tide would help us rather than hinder.

Bearing in mind the problems we had before tacking Trinity I furled away the Genoa first, but I need not have done this - Trinity came around sweet as you like and was soon on the Port tack. We hauled out the Genoa and she began to fizz. We were having a great time. Peter was helping the lads try and get a good sheeting angle and the wenches were all involved winching, and operating the running backstays. We began to overhaul large mono hulls, to windward! Trinity was pointing up to about 40 degrees of apparent wind, not quite as good as a good mono hull, but what she gave in degrees she took back in shear speed. Once more I winkled Richard from out of below to witness Trinity in full awesome romp mode. He looked pleased, but in his place I would have been gloating insufferably! Trinity was now a windward machine.

All too soon we were back at the entrance of the Hamble and stowing the sails. The electric drive pods were lowered and we made our way up the river, first of all with both generators on but I needed them off for coming alongside because I could not relate what the drives were doing with what I was doing with the throttle control on account to the engine note not changing when I operated it.

I found Trinity very difficult to get alongside smoothly; there was very little help from the paddle wheel effect when I went astern and it took a few goes before I found the answer. What worked best was backing off until I had a good bit of distance, coming in at a steep angle then putting the wheel hard over to make her skid then she would keep the turn going. If I stopped her with the outside drive going astern we arrived at the pontoon stopped and someone could step ashore with a stern spring and drop it on a cleat. I'd then go ahead gently with the outside drive keeping us pinned to the dock while we sorted the other ropes out.

Once all was sorted and everything put away I could sit down with Richard for a debrief. He asked me what I thought of the changes. I told him I was very impressed with Trinity's performance, but there was more to come. I was not happy with the sheeting arrangements for the Genoa or the staysail. Also the mainsail halliard had far too much friction in it, and the mast steps at the top of the mast had to have lashings on them to stop the halliard wrapping around them at any opportunity. The other thing the poor yacht needed was a very good clean inside. Richard booked me for an additional day to do some work on her. Then we got into Peter's car and he drove us back dropping Helen and I in Basildon and Richard in North London.

Chapter 26.

Thankfully, my diary was starting to fill up. An old customer rang me and asked me if I could deliver a small Westerly Cirrus from Gosport to Ramsgate, he had just bought the boat on eBay at a knockdown price. I told him if it was in working order I would do it, but I did not have time to do repairs. He agreed to have it fully functioning by the time got down there. My old mate Graham Smith had also been buying yacht bargains, and was now the proud owner of a Trapper 500, in Falmouth that had to be sailed up. I looked at the tides and the weather, and for once it all looked surprisingly good.

Dave the Squaddie had a great Olympics and made a fortune, getting £10 per hour for sleeping eighteen hours a day in his recovery truck. He now had some holiday to take and he called me to ask if I had any sailing trips planned! His timing was perfect. I arranged to meet him at Waterloo station the next Friday morning to catch the first train to the Hamble.

I arrived at the station and at once picked out his large powerful figure waiting for me by a camouflaged holdall. Although he left the army many years ago he is one of those ex-service men who really enjoyed their time in the forces and it shows in his demeanour. We boarded the train after getting some coffee and chewed over old times as despatch riders, having both worked in the same outfit at one time. After we had exhausted that subject we went onto boats, and he reminded me of when I had taken him sailing ten years ago and not long into the sail I had passed him the tiller and gone off to make bacon butties. Well it must have been a good sail because he had just bought a 30-foot yacht, although it was not in the water yet. Dave desperately wanted me to teach him to sail.

The plan was to do spend a day working on Trinity then go over to Gosport to do the checks on the Westerly Cirrus. I had already done the passage plan, and if we left Gosport at about 04.00 on Saturday morning we should have a good passage up to Ramsgate over the next 24 hours and be getting in there sometime on Sunday morning. I was not expecting a fast passage because the wind was forecasted to be light from the S.W. Dave would then have to go back to work and Graham Smith would pick me up on Tuesday morning from Basildon. We would drive down to Falmouth, spend the rest of the day sorting out his new purchase, and on Wednesday morning we would sail it back to Gosport. After that I had another booking for Trinity, working on her during the Friday and then do more sea trails on Saturday Sunday. A good plan - what could possibly go wrong?!

We had a long walk from Hamble station to Hamble point mariner, but it was fun as Dave has the ability to make any task humorous. We "yomped" the distance in the spirit of the Falklands heroes and it did not take long at all. Trinity impressed Dave immensely. She certainly does have a visual impact and the main cabin had been given a makeover in white leather and white during her long refit. We spent the day cleaning and tiding up. During the afternoon I rang the former owner of the Cirrus to find out exactly where she was. He answered and asked me where I was, after which he kindly offered to drive us around for £15. As this was a lot cheaper than the taxi fare I agreed. 17.00 hrs was the agreed pick up time.

He was as good as his word and showed up on time with his wife and a big 4-wheel drive. He climbed aboard and he told us about the boat, and the whole sorry sager of the over-heating problem. The first time he had sold the yacht he had ended up giving the purchaser his money back because of this problem. Then after employing a marine engineer to sort the motor out he was so desperate to be rid of what had become mill stone around his neck after he had bought another yacht, that he put it up for auction on eBay. The new owner who was employing me had "won" it for less than half of the original sale price. As we closed with Gosport he dropped his bombshell, "of course you boys know you have to take it away tonight don't you?" I asked him "why?", as we were planning to do some checks and leave at 04.00 the next morning. "it's in a MOD member only mariner, the MOD police come around and check, if they find you there you will spend the rest of the night in the cells!" I did not have time to spare to be locked up, and at this point I was tempted to tell him to turn around and take us back to Trinity. However, I wanted to see the boat so we stopped at a chippy, Dave got some dinner for us and I bought some fresh milk, bacon and bread.

We arrived shortly after that. The poor yacht had seen much better days. It reminded me of the book "Black Beauty" when the once proud horse had eventually ended up pulling a hackney carriage one step from the knacker's yard. Getting sold on eBay as a yacht is fairly low. Obviously after getting a low price, the previous owner had stripped the yacht of everything not on the inventory. A rapid look revealed empty spaces were vital items of equipment such as the cooker, echo sounder and compass had once resided. He was of course entitled to do this, but I found myself getting more than a little annoyed that this man had listened to me rattling off the passage plan knowing that the yacht was in a far from sea worthy condition. His next statement made me really cross, "of course, you know once you take it away you cannot bring it back". He said with a smirk. I was annoyed, and my irritation led me to act rashly. I knew at that point I should have found a taxi and gone back to Trinity but bearing the perfect weather forecast in mind I was loath to abandon the job. Not only was I very short of time but Dave only had a couple of days before he had to go back to work, I did not want to disappoint him. I tried the motor, which started up easily, and settled down quickly to a smooth tick over. Looking at my watch and I realised we had time to make the tidal gate at the Looe channel if we left immediately. So I told Dave to chuck the ropes off and we departed, much to the previous owner's surprise - well at least it wiped the smug look off his face anyway.

I had time to take stock of our situation as we plugged doggedly into the flooding tide out of Portsmouth. Firstly, there was, as I mentioned, a distinct lack of equipment as the yacht had been comprehensibly stripped. Along with no cooker, echo sounder, GPS, compass, spare ropes or even cups or cutlery as I had a hurried look around. The good points were a brand new VHF radio put in by the new owner. He had also left a big plastic box of goodies in a bunk, I opened it up and found a used chart plotter (he had told me it was in the box, but he had not had time to fit it). It was a relief to find it there and a rapid bit of screwing soon had it mounted on a bulkhead that could be seen from the helm station, I connected it on the same circuit as the VHF and glory be, it fired up and locked in, displaying a compass course as well as our location. There was no chart in it of course, but you can't have everything!

I then turned my attention to the sails. The main was probably the 40 year original, and over the years it had lost its battens as well as most of its shape. The "genoa" (I use the term loosely) was from a much smaller yacht and did not fit very well. In an effort to get our speed up I hoisted both and sheeted them in. We did move a little faster but not by much, and then the engine alarm went off. I shut it down and found it was running a little hot. I checked the impeller, which was ok, checked the water flow, which was also good, at which point the thermostat became the prime suspect. I always carry a basic tool kit on deliveries, but the nuts I needed to shift would not yield to an open ended flat spanner, they needed a socket spanner which I did not have. So I could not inspect it.

After its rest the engine was cooler so we started it up again at lower revs, it pushed us along at 3 knots with the "sails" up, although this was not quick enough for me as we were due to lose the tide and I wanted to get clear of the Looe channel before that happened.

Dave made the tea using the camping stove I had brought. It needed to be held still while it boiled a kettle. I was expecting some moaning about our slow progress and the state of the boat, but he, poor fool was enjoying the challenge. He remarked that the trip was becoming a lesson in all the things that could go wrong in a lifetime of sailing crammed into one short course.

We drank our tea and tucked into some of the goodies that Colin the new owner had been good enough to put in the big plastic box - lots of chocolate and stuff. I almost suffered a sense of humour loss at about 23.00 hrs. We had made it past the buoys marking the Looe channel, but a mile past we were almost stopped by the tide that had changed, and then the engine began to smell hot although the alarm had not gone off. I stopped it and we started to be swept back towards the buoys by the foul tide. I put the anchor down, at the end of its minimal chain it failed to dig in, not enough scope. I went below (after putting lots of turns of the chain around the main cleat) and attempted to release the shackle securing the bitter end beneath the fore cabin's sole. It was seized solid and very difficult to shift, my ear was pressed hard against the hull and the rumble of the dragging anchor was therefore very loud. In the end the shackle pin snapped and I released the bloody thing. Topside I added to the scope the two mooring lines and that was enough to allow the pick to dig in and we stopped. This was fortunate, because the mooring lines were the only other spare ropes on the boat!

An inspection of the engine showed that the wiring loom had fallen out of its connection at the back of the engine which was why the alarm did not go off. I put it back and pulled down the sails, and once I was convinced we were truly at a standstill, we got some rest.

At about 04.00hrs there was a little wind and the tide had eased off, so I started the engine, raised the sails and we got underway. I decided that Brighton was a good destination for repairs and we crept towards it under a sky that soon became inked in with the orange glow of a glorious sunrise. Bacon butties and strong tea raised our morale and gradually all worries and doubts were erased by a feeling of wellbeing and thankfulness to be afloat on such a wonderful morning.

The slight zephyr gradually faded away, the sun scorched us, and the sea turned blue. Brighton mariner slowly, agonisingly slowly, came closer. I phoned Colin and asked him to meet us there with an outboard motor and a good tool kit, which he agreed to do. He could not make it until 14.00 later that day, which was not a problem for us really.

Off Brighton marina we lost the help of the tide and our speed (I use the term loosely) dropped down on the GPS to 1.2 knots. We crawled through the entrance and got tied up. The new owner arrived with a brand new 9 hp outboard and a big can of fuel. He had borrowed it from a mate and asked us not to use it unless absolutely necessary, as his mate was trying to sell it. He also had a big tool kit. In next to no time I had the thermostat out and Dave pointed out that it was what those in the trade called "f##ked). The engine fired up minus this piece of useless junk and ran sweetly. The owner pointed out a large amount of weed that was hanging off the propeller (now visible for the first time in the clear water). I donned the divers mask and snorkel that I always carry on delivery trips and slipped into the water. The prop was a ball of weed and barnacles. I started cutting it free. It was taking a time so I came up for air, some marina staff in a dory started shouting at me to get out the water, I ignored them and submerged for another go and got the prop cleared and scraped of sea life.

Climbing out I was pleased not to get a bolloxing from the marina staff, I think they were just doing their health and safety duties. They knew it was nonsense and so did I, but they have to go through the motions. I did have some bleeding scratches on my arms from the barnacles, that kind of thing never fails to impress boat owners you are doing a delivery for so that was not a problem. Colin had to dash off as he was taking his wife to dinner that night, but promised to phone the next day.

Dave made some grub, which we devoured. I suppose we should have hit the fleshpots of Brighton, but we were too knackered and settled for an early night and cocoa.

It's always 04.00 when a tide seems to start running fair for me, or at least stop running against me, I don't know why this is, but it's almost an axiom. That morning ran true to form and at first light we were getting ready to leave. The engine started with ease and I could definitely feel the stronger push of the clean prop. There was hardly any wind but we pulled up the mainsail anyway, to steady us, as its baggy shape would add little to the speed. Dave was enjoying himself and insisted on steering, becoming a typical "helm hog", which was fine by me. I got on with the inevitable bacon and egg butties, washed down with strong "English breakfast" tea. There can be fewer grander ways to start a day. Things became even better, we managed to hold the fair tide all up the coast, making use of the flooding tide off the south coast, and catching the ebbing tide from the North-sea somewhere off Dungeness. Dave even found us some wind and we broad reached with as much as 7 knots on the GPS at one point. The engine ran like a sewing machine and sipped diesel in minute quantities. For a short time, I thought that we might make Ramsgate with a fair tide all the way, but it was not to be. Off Dover we began to slow drastically. It was going to be a close run thing, but I knew that if we could make it past the South Foreland we could sneak up the inside passage off Deal and cheat the foul tide. If not, we would have to put into Dover. In that case, Dave would be late for work, and I would be hard put to make my next commitment. So it was with great satisfaction that we noted our speed did not fall below 4 knots and we closed rapidly with the pier off Deal.

We could have used an echo sounder, which would have made the next few hours a lot more comfortable and less full of worry for me. I do like the Ramsgate Passage - it's such a handy route. The shallow water robs the tide of its power and users of it have an easy route into Ramsgate, but you do have to pay attention to the buoyage. We strayed from the channel and were rewarded by a slight "bump" from the nearby Brake sand bar, but it did not stop us. The light faded quickly and I was able to point out the by now dark patch of the exposed sand. Dave was impressed by how they had just appeared out of what he had thought was clear water. Back in the channel our stately progress continued, and soon it was time to call Ramsgate harbour control to request entrance. We were told to come on in. I I coached Dave in the gentle art of steering across a strong tide in darkness. Dave soon had the knack and brought us into the harbour mouth. I took over then and put us into a marina berth, next to another Westerly Cirrus.

I called Colin and told him we were safely moored up and he said he would be down the next morning. I also could not resist calling the previous owner and telling him of our safe arrival. I swear I could hear him gnashing his teeth in frustration as I told him the engine cooling problem was just a non-functioning thermostat and easily fixed. Dave called a mate and bullied him into driving down to pick him up, he left, but not before shaking my hand and thanking me for a great sailing lesson!

It was peaceful back on board. I did some tidying up and went to sleep, and awoke to a tranquil morning and good daylight. The other Cirrus had left a little earlier. I did hear it go but was too snug to move at the time. I crawled out of bed and got busy with breakfast and the first cup of tea, then finished putting the boat to rights. As a yacht she had grown on me during our trip. The engine (a small Volvo) was very good and pushed us along nicely, not using very much fuel while it did it. With a bit of fixing up and a new set of sails she would become a very steady useful little yacht.

Colin showed up and I made coffee, we had a talk and he paid me for my time and expenses. He was also kind enough to give me a lift to the train station.

Chapter 27.

On Monday I had a relaxing day with Helen, who was a bit miffed because I had hardly seen her all week was about to go off again the next day. However, she agreed to come down to the Hamble on the Saturday/Sunday to help me Take Trinity for another sail with Richard. I managed to take Boss (Helen's son's Staffordshire bull terrier) for a long walk in the woods, catch up with my post and that was the day gone, so it was time to get ready for the next couple of trips.

Graham Smith called for me at (you guessed it) 04.00. He had hired an estate car and it was overwhelmingly full, but he made just enough space so I could get in and we were Falmouth bound. Graham had just finished work, having been on nights all week, so I took over the driving after the first services. He had to put up with my sticking to the legal limits. Which if you know me is bizarre - when I rode motorbikes for a living I used to see the speed limits as challenge. I must have grown up a bit (just a little) - you still get there, not very much slower over the course of a long trip.

We arrived in the early afternoon, saw the broker and found the yacht. Our first problem was finding a place near the marina to park and unload, but all was accomplished eventually. Then the hire car was collected from us, all very stress free. We got to work, and there was plenty to do. First of all the things to do was to stow all the stuff that Graham had brought. Graham has been a delivery skipper himself and the he immediately got stuck into changing the fuel filter. Once done he expressed concern about the amount of crap that was in the fuel filter. After he had cleaned up we went off to get spare fuel filters. We hit our first snag - the chandlers only had a few in stock. Graham bought them all, along with some other bits and pieces. He also attempted to buy a spinnaker pole that was leaning against a wall, but it was not for sale. We subsequently went to various shops to try and buy a long pole to make spinnaker pole out of, but nothing we could find was suitable. The reason we needed a pole was that the forecasted winds were all westerly, and as trapper had two forestays, it would be nice to run under the two headsails all the way up to the Solent.

I routed around and found a couple of short poles lashed on the coach roof. I cut the end of the aluminium tube one off and it was big enough to stuff the other wooden one inside. I found some longish 6mm bolts and through-bolted them to keep the whole thing stable. Although I did not have a proper fitting for the mast end I passed a bit of thin nylon rope around it a few times and found a way of lashing it to keep it in place when in use. Graham was sceptical of it lasting any length of time. We went off for fuel. The Trapper's engine was small at only 8 HP single cylinder Yanmar, but just about adequate. By then I'd had a good look around, and I had to admit Graham had bagged himself a bargain. The sails were all good and although the headsails had to be hanked on I saw no reason to hold that against the yacht. She had obviously been well loved by her last owner, and I looked forward to our coming sail.

Once we refuelled we cleaned up and Graham took us off for dinner and a couple of pints. One of the local pubs served us up a couple of good steak dinners and we washed them down with "Doom Bar" - a good beer in my considered opinion. We made it back on board well before closing time as we were both struggling to stay awake. How different from my days as a fisherman out of Plymouth. I remembered one particular night. We had pulled into Falmouth after a couple of days at sea, although I was skipper of a fifty-foot trawler I had to prove how old I was because the bar staff did not believe I was legally entitled to drink. Me and my crew were young, relatively wealthy and had a lot of steam to let off, and so it was a wild night. How things had changed! Certainly no-one could have accused us that night of being anything other than respectable.

For once it was not an early start. We had time to go shopping before making a leisurely exit at about 09.00. Once clear of the marina I hoisted the main, and hanked on a number 2 genoa - she leaned to the wind and was off. Such a good mannered yacht! Clearing the harbour, our course became dead downwind so I stowed he main and hoisted the other number two and held the weather sail open with my home made pole. Graham had to eat his words, because it worked just fine. I cooked breakfast, while Graham moaned about the lack of directional stability, saying "I wish I had taken her for a test sail." I accused him of being spoilt, and after a bit of conversation it turned out that he had gotten used to sailing 40 foot yachts around, and therefore was used that level of performance. I pointed out we were hacking along at 6 to 7 knots on a waterline length of 23 foot, you can't complain about that in a lumpy sea! He had to agree, and we hammered on. Our only problem was a dead sperm whale we had to avoid, it was marked by hundreds of lucky shrieking seagulls. I was glad we did not hit it, as the smell was overpowering even from hundreds of yards away. And had we of collided with it, and it had sunk us, we would have had to make use of it as a life raft, because we did not have one aboard.

Our wonderful Westerly wind died off that night, but it had pushed us all the way to Lime Bay so we could not complain. The batteries needed a charge anyway so we ran the engine but sadly, after a couple of hours it started to splutter. Graham climbed into the starboard cockpit locker after we had emptied it, and changed the filter for a new one. The engine ran cleanly again for a few hours, then it again started to splutter. "It's no good, the fuels all contaminated" he said, the only thing we could do was take the fuel tank out and drain it to get rid of the rubbish. This took quite a time but Graham accomplished it with the minimum of swear words. Once done, the engine ran again for another few hours, and then started to splutter again. Graham was not a very happy bunny; "I am allergic to diesel you know" he muttered as once more he crawled into the tiny space in the cockpit locker to change the filter. It was our last one. We prayed for more wind. Dawn found us just passing Portland Bill, but then with a very poorly engine and not a lot of wind, our progress was slow. I was all too aware that we had to be in Gosport that night for me to keep my appointment with Richard and Trinity in the Hamble the next day.

Over the course of the day we worked our way to the mouth of the Solent, but the tide was due to turn at 16,00 and it was nearly that time already. As the wind was falling even lighter it was time to play my joker. Or more exactly use my "phone a friend" option. My very good pal, Chris Lewis who runs the ferry service in the river Medina from Island marina to east and west Cowes. I called him up and explained our predicament. "No problem Max, I will bring some filters and a spare bit of fuel line out to you." That is the kind of mate he is! Meanwhile back on the yacht my home made spinnaker pole was doing sterling service and the sails were pushing us slowly over the fast running tide. A surprisingly short time later we received a call on the radio; it was Cath, Chris's better half. They had borrowed a fast RIB and had our filters. Graham was stunned, because we were still miles from anywhere really. I handed over some cash, obviously not enough for service like that, but some weeks later I was able to go some way towards repaying Chris's kindness.

With the filters aboard we went off to find someplace to anchor. We should have headed towards Limington until we found shoal water, but in a mad moment we crossed the Solent and battled with the tide not to get swept out towards the needles. There was a small yacht amongst the rocks and obviously out of the tide. It was by a castle, and we found 15 foot of water and dropped the hook. While we once more emptied the cockpit locker to change the filter we found we were witnessing a RNLI rescue! The yacht we had seen was not a cunning local anchored in a deep water pool, but someone who had tacked in and run aground, on rocks, with a falling tide. Various RNLI boats showed up after a launch attempted to tow the yacht off. It was no go, and the people were taken off. Thankfully, we were having a bit more success.

Our filter replaced with a nice new virgin one, we decided to stay anchored until the tide changed and make Gosport at about, 02.00. We had a bite and a bit of rest. Then at about 22.00, the tide eased. There was little wind but the motor started smoothly, so I pulled up the anchor, Graham engaged forward gear, at which point the motor promptly died. I hoisted the sails, while Graham started emptying the cockpit locker again, swearing horribly and once more reminding me that he was allergic to diesel. Fortunately, the Trapper 500 sails on the merest waft of air in flat water so I was able to keep her going in the right direction while Graham worked his air bleeding magic. It was a good night for a motor sail and apart from my cunning short cut across the sands off Portsmouth that had the echo sounder down to 1.5 meters for a very long 15 minutes, uneventful.

We went in and attempted to pick up a mooring near the ferry terminal, of which there were none that were un-occupied, and then the engine once more died. No wind at all so I dropped the hook and we stopped. Of course we could not dig the pick in because we could not go astern, but with no wind and no tide it did not seem a problem to two very tired guys, we were in about 10 foot of water so it an appropriate moment to have a very short sleep. It seemed like my head had just hit the pillow when I heard a knocking noise, by my ear. I hit the deck like scalded cat, to find we were berthed nicely alongside the ferry terminal! Graham was just as amused as I was. I pulled in the anchor that was hanging straight down into the much deeper water. Graham tried the engine and it started, at once and ran sweetly. We motored into the marina and found an empty finger berth, by then it was that magic hour 04.00, I was grateful to return to my bunk.

Chapter 28

I awoke at 08.00, got my kit together and after a welcome brew walked over to the taxi rank near the entrance to the marina. I asked the driver to take me to Hamble point marina. Once there I became a customer of the Ketch bar and ordered a bacon sandwich accompanied by a mug of tea, it was very nice but eye-wateringly expensive.

After climbing aboard Trinity I started the work on the first thing on my list - cleaning up the aft cabin. The engineer Richard had booked arrived not long after and I worked with him to get the port engine running. He showed me the button that had to be pressed to get it to bleed. The generators had electric fuel pumps and the system had to be bypassed to bleed the air from the lines. I had never come across that system before. Once he had done his job and left I went onto re rigging the staysail sheeting points.

My day was brightened when Helen showed up in the evening, and I took her for a meal in the Ketch rigger bar. Very good it was too.

Richard arrived the next day and we continued working on Trinity to get her ready for the sail on Sunday. The plan at that time was to do a circumnavigation, anticlockwise of the isle of wright. About 16.00 Richard noticed there was a bit of play on the port tiller. He went below to investigate, and shortly afterwards he called me down to look at what he had found. The port hydraulic ram had been put on with two self-tapping screws! It was the same on the other side. Obviously we could not sail with the steering in that state. Richard fortunately had some long 8 mm bolts with washes that would serve, but we had no drill. I was despatched in a taxi to the local B&Q, in a neat coincidence the taxi driver had also just recently purchased a battery drill from B&Q and as he was one of those kind of people who really goes into things, on the ride there I was educated into which drill was best for the money. I came back with a Bosch drill and a suitable pack of drill bits.

The job to drill the holes in a very confined space and bolt down the rams took until 22.30, at which point I told Richard I was going to bed, and he was still working on the electrics when I said "goodnight".

My passage plan called for a very early start, but the weather was not suitable for an untried yacht to attempt a circumnavigation of the Isle of Wight so we did not get going until way past 09.00, I decided to go West down the Solent, into the wind, and also the building tide. It certainly was a good test of Trinity's new found windward ability. As we hit 8 knots, we pulled the Starboard outdrive out of the water, then went to raise the port one. We hit a problem - it was half off its bracket and jammed in the space. We could see what had failed, it was only attached by two thumb screws, there was a facility to bolt it to the bracket but someone had used self-tapping screws instead of bolts, and these had fallen out. I could see that a theme was developing here! I heaved Trinity too, which she did very well, and we man handled the drive back onto its bracket and Richard found some bigger self-tappers that we used to make it a bit secure, then we raised it out of the water.

There were several yacht races going on that Sunday morning, and we went hunting mono hulls, the grand old lady "Sceptre " came past us, to leeward, we gave chase and our hull speed in 16 knots of wind was very close to hers, but she was out pointing us and gradually drew away, then we got into a pack of hard sailed 34 foot yachts, again our hull speed was about the same, suddenly the wind gusted up to 22 knots, and the mono hulls leaned a lot more despite the crew members lining their weather rails, but Trinity did not lean, well maybe slightly, and she used the extra power to surge forward. The GPS was suddenly reading 10.5 knots, that was into the tide, and the mono hulls where falling rapidly behind us! The wake we were leaving was like the rooster tails some power boats leave, it was awesome. Richard had the wheel and for the first time I saw a definite smile on his face. He wanted to carry on and go past Hurst, but despite what some people may think I am a cautious sailor, I was still not convinced that Trinity was ready for the open sea. We spent another hour or so tacking about at different angles to the wind and playing with the genoa sheet leads, I was still not happy about the forestay tension, but Trinity was improving all the time.

Helen took the wheel and Richard and I worked the sheets to gybe. It all went off smoothly enough and soon we were broad reaching with the tide back up the Solent. After the windward work of progress seemed very sedate, but we rapidly ate up the distance back to Southampton water. Then we were off Hamble point and it was time to drop the sails, and also the drives so we could motor. I took it very easy with the power, as the last thing I wanted was to be towing an electric drive pod on a cable underneath the yacht.

Once safely berthed we had tea and while Helen cooked a meal we had a debrief. We had a long talk; Trinity was obviously becoming a sailing machine with awesome potential, but she still needed someone to rectify all her small problems and sort out the bigger issues. Richard asked me if I would do it, I told him I would have to have some help, at which point he agreed that I could hire someone to assist me. We ate our pizza and planned out our next move. I could work on some of the smaller issues the next day, but I still had the Trapper in Gosport to help get back to Thurrock Yacht Club, and for Helen's birthday I had bought tickets for a tour of Buckingham palace, and that was the next week end. So we agreed I would start the serious stuff on Monday week, meanwhile I would hunt up an assistant.

After all this Helen left with Richard to catch the train back to London. I hit the phone, first call was to my old mate Chris Lewis who had so recently saved my bacon with the fuel filter delivery hoping that I could repay his kindness. I asked him if he wanted the work, but he was too busy, but he had a mate who lived on the island who had helped him out on several occasions, who like Chris was an ex hovercraft engineer, he gave me his number. That was the first time I spoke to Andy Pavey. I told him that we needed someone to first of all completely re-plumb the water system on Trinity and then help me tackle the other jobs that needed doing; all-in-all there was about three week's work. There were logistical problems to be overcome, but finally we worked it out that if Andy came over in his own yacht he could carry all his tools and also have his accommodation problem sorted too, and he could also keep his yacht in the marina. We agreed that he would show up on Tuesday week.

With this all sorted, I got some sleep. In the morning I started work on the various small water leaks, and then removed the Bow roller and Pulpit. Both items needed to be redesigned; the pulpit because the feet were not long enough to be able to bolt it down properly, and the bow roller because it was too short for an anchor to sit in it properly. It was difficult to get both items off without damaging the hull, or dropping them over the side, but it was accomplished. I then started work on the auto pilot that was refusing its duty. I found it had not been set up properly and with the manual went through the steps. It started working and went hard to starboard then port a few times before locking solid on starboard helm. I investigated and found another horror story - Trinity used to have a middle rudder that had been removed in the big refit, but the ram had been left in place still connected to the system, and after a few cycles it would be out of phase with the other the two rams and would lock up on starboard. Obviously it had to be taken out. I phoned up hydraulic engineers in the area and two agreed to show up on Tuesday week to give me a quote. While they were at it I wanted to move the auto pilot motor into the engine room. After all this I had a meal and got some more rest, to ready myself for the sail to come. The weather looked like it was going to degrade and blow hard from the West on Wednesday, the same day we would be bashing up the Thames Estuary.

Chapter 29

Another early morning taxi ride took me to Gosport and Graham Smith's trapper. He looked a lot more relaxed than last time I had seen him, he had renewed a lot of the fuel system and given the tank a very good clean out. His wife and kids had been down for the week end and they had enjoyed the new yacht. We got going and Graham fitted the tiller pilot he had found in one of the bunks - glory be, it worked and kept us on track nicely. We had to motor sail quite a bit but covered the ground quickly and next morning we were off Dover. Graham decided to put in and wait out the tide that was about to go foul. We tied up on the waiting pontoon and cheekily used the shower facilities without paying for a berth, ducking in when another chap came out. Then we went over to the café and had breakfast. After that we went off to the fuel berth and filled up, to our amazement we only needed a couple of gallons, as the 8 HP Yanmar was just sipping the stuff.

The fuel berth man pointed out the tide was flowing in our favour by then, I think he wanted us gone, but I pointed out that if we left too early, sure we would get the North-sea ebb to the Estuary, but then we would be stopped by the Thames estuary Ebb, then since the wind was forecasted to be Westerly force 7 we would be stuffed.

The wind obviously had not read the forecast and was still light and from the South West so we stayed another hour or so then left, with just the number 2 genoa set. We hurtled up past Ramsgate carried nicely by the tide, we wanted to take our time, but the Trapper was having none of it and insisted in gobbling up the miles despite only having up the headsail. In consequence we arrived at the Prince's Channel about an hour too early, of course the wind took that moment to swing into the West and blow the promised force 7. I dropped the headsail, Graham started the engine, to hold us into the wind while I hoisted the main sail with its biggest reef, and then the working jib. Once all snugged down the Trapper was comfortable but we were still losing ground. It was like a welcome home, especially when the cold rain started - how many times I had been in that situation in the Thames, battering in to a fast running tide, pinching up trying to get a lee bow and not get swept backwards into shoal water or a navigation Buoy. Graham suggested running back to Ramsgate but I told him we were in the ideal place, when the tide turned, which it would, we would make ground through the channel and pick up a better wind angle. I called up a ship that was wondering what we were doing, and told him we would stay out of his way. We served out our hour or so of purgatory, then the wind swung back to the South West the rain stopped and the tide slacked off so we could make up the channel.

The wind dropped off more and more so I took in the fore sail and un-reefed the main and the motor pushed us on into the darkness off Leigh on Sea. A black shape materialised into a RIB manned with serious looking armed cops, one came aboard and interrogated us to find out if we were terrorists or drug runners, once Graham had convinced them that we were neither they let us carry on. We reached Thurrock Yacht Club moorings with the last of the fair tide, picked one up and gratefully crept into our sleeping bags - it had been a long day.

The big clean-up started at about 08.00, after of course tea and bacon sarnies. Graham was now expressing his pleasure at Barakat's performance, for a small yacht she had done very well and averaging more than 110 miles per 24 hours consistently. Once we had her looking shipshape we inflated Graham's tiny inflatable and overloading it with ourselves and our gear, made a very wet passage back to the yacht club where we waited for Sue (Graham's better half) to pick us up.

Job done I had a well-deserved day off before spending the next day with Helen in Buckingham palace, I must admit to enjoying it far more than I thought I would. I was also impressed by how well the whole thing was conducted - we were made to feel like important honoured guests. We also went to Number 1 London, which was the Duke of Wellington's residence, as I have always wanted to visit there. We walked in had a good look around and walked out, and as we made our exit I realised we were supposed to have paid. We didn't and had that delicious naughty feeling that makes children giggle. A good lunch and then the train home - it was a wonderful day, twice as sweet for the contrast of my recent activities, and the fact that I would be away again the next day.

Chapter 30

Saturday saw me on the train back to the Hamble. I spent two days working on Trinity before Andy showed up on Monday morning. He sailed up, and I saw him taking in his main, before motoring gently over to pass me his lines, as soon as I saw the way he handled his yacht, I knew we were going to get on. Andy had started his working life as an apprentice in a factory that made aircraft, he was a fastidious engineer, but a steady worker. We complimented each other perfectly and soon cracked into the various jobs that had to be done. Richard had commissioned a survey for the steering system - the survey had condemned the whole set up as being very badly put together and not safe to go on any further sea trials with. All the various parts needed proper backing plates fitted and the whole thing needed "tuning". Once Andy had replaced all the plumbing we started on that, we had been working a few days when a worker from the very expensive yard who had fitted the steering system showed up, and without a word walked past us and onto Trinity, I asked him what he wanted, he said "I am here to sort the steering out" I told him as far as I was concerned his company had committed an act of treason with the work they had done and I did not trust them to do any more, and would he get off Trinity. He left, without saying anything.

Richard had already measured up for the backing plates we needed, and it was just a case of chasing up the fabricators to get them made. Richard came down with the bolts he had ordered and I got on with fitting them. The marine architect Doug Hinge arrived to look at a few things and I had a chance to talk to him, and while we were standing on the bow of the main hull he said to me "she is very lightly built you know." I told him I would be very careful not to hit anything. I had a long discussion with him and Richard. That is when I first heard that there was a problem with how Trinity had been built. She was of epoxy, ply, and foam sandwich construction. But the wrong foam had been used, and that in a survey delamination of the outer skin on the outer hulls had been found. A "cure" had been tried, at great expense the outer hulls had been sheathed in epoxy and glass cloth. Sadly, although this had handled the weakness below the waterline, it had added 1.5 tons of weight. Because of this and all the added equipment Trinity was well down on her marks. At the same time because the bad foam had not been taken out, above the waterline she was still very weak in places, and any kind of impact could cause local delamination.

This was all a bit worrying but my gut feeling was that Trinity was very strong - when we sailed her she felt "stiff", and not weak at all. For instance, the rigging never went slack. For all the extra weight, she was a fast yacht and very pleasant to sail. At the time I thought that a big weight saving program would be the best way forward.

Richard and the architect were discussing ways of making some kind of drive pod lifting device, the way we had to deploy them at that time was time consuming and took two people, one had to use a rope to take the weight and the other attempted to pull out a pin. As it was stainless steel going into aluminium it was usually corroded and had to be wiggled with pliers before it would move. Once it was pulled back the pod could be lowered.

They both left a little later and Andy and I got on with our work. We worked out a way of deploying and recovering the electric drives by utilising a couple of dinghy kicking strap tackles. It worked brilliantly and saved making a far more complicated set up - now one person could easily raise or lower a drive pod. Later that evening I did a test. There was a board that was used as part of the deck in the engine room - it was constructed in the same way as the hull was, epoxy glass cloth, plywood, polystyrene, plywood glass epoxy. I put it on two bits of wood and jumped on it, it did break in the end, but it was reassuringly difficult to do.

After totally re-plumbing Trinity and getting rid of the plastic snap together system that kept snapping apart and dumping the water, Andy helped me disassemble the steering. I drilled the holes and fitted the back plates. He worked on making everything run true. Some of the howlers we found were that a bulk head had not been continued up to the deck in both hulls near the stern, because there was a sort of "letterbox" opening in the sterns for the steering rods, this meant there was an opening that the sea could get in and flood each hull. Another really stupid thing was that the end rod bearings were made from ordinary hardened steel; they were already rusty and seizing up with just one sail! Andy also found that one of them was held on with just 3 threads. We also had to replace most of the bolts because the ones fitted were too short and just came undone, because there was not room to fit washers.

The list of stupid things went on and I found myself getting very cross about the situation. But the straw that broke the camel's back was the forward bilge pump. We had another test sail and the forward bilge filled up. I switched the electric pump on and cleared it, but it filled up again quite quickly, so I kept the pump running until we reached the marina. When I went to find the leak, I could not see any water coming in anywhere. Then I realised that the bilge pump was fitted right at the bottom of the bilge, and the pipe was just a little way above it, the outlet was only just above the waterline, when Trinity was moving the bow wave went above this, the tiny little non return valve was jammed open with a bit of electric wire insulation, so the water could run into the bow and flood that chamber! These guys had charged Richard top money for this work, so I wrote the man I had been told who was in overall charge an email, and in it I told him what I thought of his firm's workmanship. After I had sent it I was still cross, so I went over to see him.

Walking into the office I asked to see this character, the receptionist pointed to him sitting behind a desk, there were a couple of smartly dressed men standing around, I interrupted them, and introduced myself, I did not offer my hand. The guy looked at me and said "I hear you have been saying bad things about me in the marina" I said "yes, now I am here to say it to your face, how dare you send me to sea with a yacht that was about to lose its steering and that was in a condition that it would flood, and how come your comedians could not even install the forward bilge pump properly?", the smartly dressed men around him melted away. There were a few excuses, and then he said "Richard has some stuff stored here, I will show you where it is, follow me". I expected a fight to start, and he wanted me in the warehouse, but no, there really was stuff that had to be moved onto Trinity. I found it unbelievable that someone could run a company that surely must protect its reputation could afford to have me talking like that in the office without doing anything to make things right, but no, it seemed like they really did not care. I told him I would move the stuff, and left.

Chapter 31

About this time Richard called the original builder over, who had heard he had been having a bad time of things and wanted to give him Trinity's old sails - that's how I met the Dutchman. My first impression of him was not good. He came on-board while I and Andy were working. He was tall well-built and very confident, with long flowing blond hair. Something inside me wanted to slap him, funnily enough now I look back on the situation I wish I had done so, as it would have saved a lot of grief. Trinity had been the first boat that he had built. My dad has a saying, "the first boat you build, you give it to your enemies, the second, you sell, and you keep the third". How true this saying is, I was soon to find out, because despite the wonderful finish inside and the really clever design features, she was a ticking time bomb.

The Dutchman stayed on the boat that night and I had a chance to have a long discussion with him about how the boat was constructed. He told me that most people including surveyors did not understand that because he had used a lot of battens when they checked for "delamination" by tapping with a mallet, the different noises they heard was the mallet hitting the batten. The story had a ring of truth to it, and like a gullible idiot, I fell for it. After all, I had done a destruction test on that part of engine room deck and it had shown itself to be strong.

The Dutchman came on a sail with Richard and me the next day. We sailed to Studland Bay, the wind was from the S.W. at first, but we had the tide to carry us tacking to windward down the Solent. Trinity was in her element; very fast and quite close winded on the flat water - all in all a joy to sail. Once off Hurst the evening wind fell light and eventually we had to turn on the electric drives. They behaved faultlessly and we powered along quietly at five knots with the tide for four hours, then one hour with the genies had the batteries fully charged up. It was becoming dark when we dropped the anchor close to the other yachts at Studland. We ate pizza and talked boats. It was all very congenial. Except that I had become a sort of "dog's body". I was running the yacht, making tea and fixing the food. I was glad it was only a short trip. After a tranquil night I cooked breakfast and made ready for sea. We did not have an early start because for once the tide was going to become fair for us at a civilised 10.30.

The forecast was for Westerly wind at about noon. When we finally did sail majestically to sea, there was a slight breeze from the West. Inside about a mile from us a mono hull race was in progress. The spinnakers came out, we pulled up our dagger boards, and found on a broad reach we could keep up with them, but the turbulence behind us was very noticeable. As the wind built, we rounded up and took in the mainsail, we slowed down and started to lose the other yachts, but I knew that when we got into the race of Hurst we would have to gybe - I did not want to be over-canvased going into the congested waters off there. We had a great sail back, and I steered most of the time because Richard and the Dutchman were deep in conversation below. They finally came out when we were of Calshott point. Something was brewing and I found out what it was when we were tied up.

"Max, how would you like to sail Trinity down to Portugal for me?" was how the owner started the conversation. It seems that the Dutchman had pointed out that although Trinity was fast and now went to windward, the weight she had put on was slowing her down. In Portugal he could cut off the outer hulls below the waterline, make them a more buoyant shape and get her back on her marks. I had another quiet conversation with the Dutchman and he was adamant that Trinity was strong and could take a Biscay crossing late in the year, so I decided to trust him.

I told Richard "Yes, providing we leave before the end of September". Time was tight and a crew had to be found. Helen did not want to come, so I needed at least 4 people. Richard was coming, so that was 3 to find. I posted an advert on "Crew seekers" and started getting replies, I put an advert on Thurrock Yacht Club's Face Book site, and I also started ringing around past crews. Little Mick could not make it, but my brother Alex said he might be able to come. I tried to find Dave the squaddie who had sailed with me a few weeks before and said he wanted to do a bigger trip, but his phone was dead. I left a message with the marina he stays at. Then Karen from our club rang and said she wanted to come if she could get time off work. And one of the answers to the ad in Crew seekers seemed suitable. So suddenly we were crewed up.

Next was the weather. To my surprise it was forecasted to play ball. The next few days would be awful, but then the next week the wind would swing into the Northerly quadrant and stay there for about 4 days - just what we needed.

I rang everybody and told them the glad news and that we would be off on the 27th and the forecast was perfect. Then Squaddie Dave got in contact, absolutely gutted that he could not come, however my brother had not been able to get the time off work after all, so Dave could come - he was very pleased.

Chapter 32

I came down the day before and started getting ready, I had a bad case of butterflies and could not sleep "what if the surveys were right and Trinity was going to delaminate and break up?" was rattling around in my head. I knew we had a good life raft an EPERB and flares, but it was still a worry.

The crew started showing up - Pete from up North, had sailed before, and wanted to do this trip to get more miles. Dave, very happy to be there arrived and was his normal really cheerful self. I sent him off to the supermarket with a big list that he and Pete (who had once been a chef) knocked up. On Dave's way back Karen called from the Hamble train station, so I had Dave pick her up in his taxi. They appeared with loads of bags and Pete and I went to help them with the carrying. Back on Trinity we started stowing stuff. Once that was done I did various drills with them, fire being the most important. I had them locate all the fire extinguishers and show me how each one worked. I had each crew member demonstrate the correct way to put out a hot fat fire with a fire blanket.

They all had a life jacket from the store and it was fitted to them. We did a man overboard drill (dry we did not leave the pontoon) then we went and got fuel up the river. My phone went just after fuelling was completed. Richard had arrived and found his yacht was gone. I told him we were on our way back to collect him.

We arrived and another yacht had pinched our berth. There was nowhere else to go that we could get alongside to pick up Richard and his bags, so we stayed close by and persuaded the yacht that it really was our berth the owner had paid thousands for, and really we could not go anywhere else and eventually he moved off. Once alongside, we had Richard on board and we left. A sense of excitement raged through the crew. I knew I was going to have my work cut out, but what they lacked in experience I was sure they would make up for with enthusiasm.

The sails were hauled up as soon as we were clear of the cardinal mark off the Hamble, the electric drives retracted and we started to sail. The tide was fair for Hurst point, the wind almost so, few tacks were needed, but that was good training so no complains there. The sun was even out and I passed the helm to Karen as we thundered down the Needles channel the chart plotter said we were doing 13 knots over the ground, Karen whooped with joy and Dave's smile became more Cheshire cat-like. Pete made sandwiches and Richard looked well happy.

Sadly the wind became more Westerly, all was not lost. I worked out we could clear Cherbourg, get down amongst the Channel Islands and then go onto the port tack to catch the ebb tide though the Alderney race. People started to go down with sea sickness; Trinity at speed in an open sea has an uncomfortable motion and poor Karen was worst affected. This was a blow, because at that point she was the best helmsman in the crew. We had a watch list, and everybody had a two hour stint, but I always had to be there, making sure the helm did not come too close to the wind. If that happened Trinity would promptly stop, and we would have to go through the wearing process of getting her back on tack and sailing again, all the time losing much needed sea room. I was getting tired by the Cape, but we successfully passed it and Peter took over the helm. I wanted to get down to Jersey before we tacked, but after Peter had put us in Irons twice I began to think he might do better if we were on the port tack, so we put about and passed Sark to Port, visible by its many lights in the darkness.

By dawn the wind had backed even more, and aided by the now foul tide we could just lay a course for Dartmouth. Karen was very ill, and cheered up when she heard the news. She was still doing her stints on the wheel, and indeed that was the only time I could rest. Later that afternoon the tide changed and we could lay a course for L'abwrack on the Brittany coast, almost where we wanted to go. I attempted to wake Karen, but she was very sound asleep. I thought that when she awoke she might be better and not too disappointed to not be going into Dartmouth.

Some hours later we fell off a wave and the fore trampolines were ripped out, leaving some large holes in the bow. I was worried at how easy the eye bolts had pulled out, taking the large washes with them; it was more than a little disconcerting. I heaved too, so we could clear the wreckage and make repairs. Down below in the bow centre section the sides could be seen to be visibly "oil canning", meaning you could see them moving in and out with the wave pressure; it's not a good sign. There was also a large amount of water in all the three bow sections, the automatic bilge pump was not working, and failed to keep up with the hatch leaks. We were taking in lots of water mostly from badly fitting hatches, also under the cockpit floor on both side, there was a big drain hole that the floor boards covered, every time a large wave hit them, water would cascade up past the floor and a good quantity would get past the stern hatches into the rear of the Amas.

While we were sorting the mess out Karen appeared, obviously less than happy to find us further away from dry land than when she went off watch. Not to mention on board a damaged vessel in a lumpy sea. Richard wanted to carry on once repairs had been made, but I felt that this would be a mistake in that should the wind back again and we could not make a safe haven, with the boat already damaged and a very sea sick crew member on board we could really put ourselves in a bad position. So I ordered a course for Dartmouth and we arrived there at 00.15 the next day.

We dropped anchor and started repairs. The fix for the holes I had made with large bolts washes and patches from the inflatable dinghy repair kit had worked well. Richard took a 24 volt deck wash pump and cleverly wired it in to make an automatic bilge pump. After an hour or so we were in a state to face the sea again, apart from the hatch leaks. Karen still wanted to go ashore, and Peter had found out that his wife had broken her ankle so he wanted to return home as well. I was reluctant to leave, but I gave the choice to Richard. He wanted to go on and take advantage of the weather forecast that was still insisting that the weather would be mostly from the North West. Accordingly, I dropped Karen and Peter off at Kingsweir and at 02.00 we put to sea. The indomitable Dave was still in good spirits.

It was a lovely night. I put Richard and Dave on the helm told them to steer the best course they could and not to pinch it up, and I went to bed. Amazingly I managed several good hours of proper sleep before coming up to find daylight and Trinity romping along towards Ushant. The sun was even out, but gradually the wind faded away and we had to use the drives to keep us moving.

It was a tranquil day that saw us pass Ushant and later on the wind filled in from the south West and I found that putting Trinity's bow slightly off it rather than hard on it allowed us to raise the out drives and sail on at a slightly faster rate for the sacrifice of a few degrees of course. The wind filled in a bit more and we started to romp. The forecast was still giving North west winds, we were still getting slightly south of West, I thought that somewhere along the route they had to get it right and so I was not too concerned that we were being set well inside of Cape Finasterre, reasoning that when we did get a wind shift we would be able to follow it round and make up the lost ground.

Dave Norman taking a well-earned sleep in the Spanish sunshine on the trimaran Trinity

Chapter 33

Thirty-six hours later we were closing the Spanish coast, lining up nicely with Gijon, 120 miles off course. The MET had lied like a cheap rug, well actually 60 miles in front of us the wind did have a Northerly component, but we could never get into it. Richard had found a site and a mobile signal that showed the current wind all down the coast. I still had my fingers crossed, but realistically the answer was to find a good port and wait until the wind went fair for us. However, Richard was on a very tight time scale and wanted to be back in the U.K. as soon as possible. We carried on. Dave wanted to go fishing so we dug out the fishing gear. Needless to say as there were two rods it turned into a competition between us, and much to my mortification the lucky git got a bite and when he pulled in his line there were three large Mackerel flapping on the line!

Dave is a master gloater, and I was getting a serious mauling when we went for a tack, somehow after the last time Dave had rigged his Rod, he had forgotten to lash it down, as we tacked and the mainsail went over, Dave's rod shot off the stern and was lost to Neptune. Richard had his back to the drama, and as Dave failed to notify him I was presented the delivery skippers dream, perfect blackmail material. So that was the end of Dave's gloat-fest.

The foul Southwest wind died off to nothing leaving a lumpy sea, we put the sails away and motored west using the electric drives, but our speed was painful as the drives were alternatively lifter clear of the water by the Tri's motion. Later that night the wind came back, from almost due west, we began tacking, at first changing tacks at every 2-hour watch change, but I began to suspect that there might be more wind offshore and maybe if we got clear of the land we might get a better slant, so we held the offshore tack all through the night. In the early hours Richard had the watch just as daylight was beginning to break, but that's not all that broke. Trinity fell off a wave there was a big bang and the starboard trampoline that is fixed behind the big carbon spar that ties all three hulls together, blew out. I heaved too. The wind was up, as was the swell, but our real problem was exposed when I lifted the after starboard hatch, the ama was half full of water, again. We started bailing and pumping, first the after compartments and then the bows. We shifted a lot of water. And rescued the trampoline, cutting the lashings to remove both of them, and stow them back in my cabin.

I looked at the chart. We were 50 miles from the nearest safe haven which was Viverro, and the wind gauge said it was gusting up to 34-36 knots while we were heaved too. But our course was slightly off the wind for the Spanish port, we could fetch it without tacking. The sea was building nicely and we would need a lot of power to drive us over it. I told Richard we had three choices, 1 run back across the Bay of Biscay to Ushant, 2/ stay heaved too until conditions changed.3 let me crack on towards Viverro. He chose option number 3. The second reef was already in the main, I let the staysail draw and we started to move, but kept getting stopped by every wave, our progress was not fast enough. So I unleashed the Genoa, only about half of it. Trinity went into overdrive, gambolling over the seas like a frisky panzer tank at 10 knots. I figured it would kill or cure us, I stayed on the helm attempting to steer around the bigger waves, Richard stayed up with me enjoying the ride and Dave tried to keep stuff from getting broken down below, passing up tea and telling me I was mad from time to time. We took the top off 4 waves in succession at one point and the large hatches in the coach roof leaked badly. It did not seem like 5 hours - time passed quickly, as it does when you're having fun, but Spain seemed to rapidly appear and get bigger. The sea and the wind died down as we approached.

The river to the marina was quite a long trek. We had to do it under motor because the wind began to funnel in the mouth, and tacking would have exposed us to the problem of hitting some of the massed fishing gear strewn about the place. It was midnight before we finally tied up. I was on my way to get some sleep when Richard suggested we start pumping the boat out, but I ordered him to bed, "Time for that in the morning" I told him. I fell at once into a deep and dreamless sleep.

I awoke and crawled from the aft cabin to find a glorious sunny morning was in full swing, Dave had also just appeared we went ashore for real coffee that we found in a local café. I attempted to find the marina office but it was shut so to get back to Trinity we had to climb over the gate. Richard woke up and we went to find some fuel, only available from the petrol station at the top of the hill. At least we came down the hill with the big load.

I also did some repairs to the mainsail, the running backstay had been taking big chunks out of the batten pockets, so the only thing I could think of to stop the brand new sails from getting totally wrecked was to put gaffer tape over the damage. It did not seem to matter how much we tried to keep the heavy stainless wire swinging across and damaging the sail, it still managed a vindictive swipe that chaffed the material.

I did eventually contact the marina manager. He said they had just taken over and were not set up to take money, so we blagged a free overnight stay. Richard took us for a bite to eat, and then at about

18.00, the wind having dropped down a few Beauforts, we departed.

It took us a while to clear the river but in a rapidly dimming evening we at last once more moved to the open sea. Once again the wind was on our nose. Thankfully the sea was down so we could use the electric drives and make our way directly towards Cape Finasterre. In the morning we were close to Corunna. I was all for going there and waiting for a proper slant but Richard wanted to press on. As there was slightly more wind we rolled out the genoa, stopping and hauling up the electric drives, commenced sailing and tacking towards our objective, Portimao in Portugal. It was hard work, but Trinity was making reasonable progress so we continued, tacking at each two-hour watch change. This meant that none of us was able to get much rest, but me least of all as I had to be there at each tack.

I had a message that good old Edmund Whelan was in the same neck of the woods so I sent him a message on my phone when we got a signal. He called back, telling me that he was stuck in Vila Garcia. Fortunately, we would be sailing past in the afternoon. He was sensibly staying put until the wind stopped blowing from where he wanted to go. I suggested that we might go and join him, but Richard was intent on getting to Portugal so as we were making progress we kept on for another 36 hours.

As I mentioned before Edmund was a very dear friend of mine, we had met on a RYA cruising instructor course several years before. I was still at that point earning a living as a Motorcycle Despatch rider in London and he had just retired from being the top Barrister at the RYA, so it was to say the least a very unlikely friendship. However, we got on very well. He had even sailed with me and another guy (captain Blood (alias Jack Vandenbroele) across the Atlantic on my old wreck of a schooner Gloria. After a long working life as a Barrister Ed now indulged his passion by teaching sailing and delivering yachts. He was amongst the finest people you could ever sail with, or indeed bump into at a bar. I was sorry not have met up with him that time.

We sailed across the invisible line that marks the Spanish/Portuguese border. Actually, you can tell because instantly the amount of fishing gear markers trebles. I had had enough of the constant battering and pointed out to Richard that the objective of getting to Portugal had been achieved and we should put into the next port which was Vivian Castello. He agreed and so just after midnight on the 7th we tied up on the waiting pontoon of the marina. We did go inside, but it was tiny and there was no place for us to safely berth. Our trip had taken 10 days to cover the roughly 1000 miles. It may not sound too good, but if you take into account that most of the trip was hard on the wind, and we had put back to Dartmouth at one point as well as heaving too for a total of at least 6 hours making repairs, plus one night off then it looks a lot better. I though Trinity had acquitted herself well; there was a world of difference in windward ability on a flat sea to windward ability in open water. With the best will in the world, in my opinion, a good cruising yacht will only really do 40-50 degrees for an extended period in any kind of sea way I don't care what the glossy magazines or the bar experts say. Trinity had been able to do this, so I was very happy with her sailing performance.

Richard was in a hurry to get back to his office, and Dave had used up all his holiday so they both left later that day. I phoned the Dutchman/boat builder who had said that he would be available to help bring Trinity to Portimao where he was going to do the work. I had to leave messages because at first I could get no answer.

He eventually called me back and we arranged for him to travel the 300 miles to join the boat, not without a fair bit of winging from him regarding how difficult it was to get to us. Looking at the weather forecast I could see that the wind would be stuck in the S.W. for a few days, so I was in no great hurry to get going. I went running, and it was good to feel solid ground under my feet again.

Chapter 34

The Dutchman arrived a couple of days later, moaning about how skint he was. We went and had a bite to eat and he helped me carry back food for our trip. We went over the forecast. I said I wanted to stay in port until we had a fair wind, but he wanted to check out Trinity's windward ability in a sea way, (when he had built her she did not have dagger boards, but short stub keels). I reluctantly agreed, so we left then next day. I started both generators to check them, or at least I attempted to. The port one would not fire up, which was a real pain because not only did the generators only charge up one set of the drive batteries each, but the port one charged up the 24 volt and 12 volt banks, and there was no way of linking them. I figured that I could get it to start later - the important thing was to get to sea, so we left. The Dutchman wanted to have a go at manoeuvring Trinity under power. He had a go at getting alongside the pontoon we had just left but found it was not as easy as he expected. He started using the port motor a lot and in the end I told him that if for some reason I could not get the dead generator to start then we would not be able to replace the power he was wasting and he stopped doing it.

Once outside we hoisted sail and put her on the wind, the Dutchman went through all the sail settings, over the next few hours changed everything, and then changed them all back to how I had it set up. I was starting to get a little annoyed. He also told me that he did not cook at sea. Fine, I told him, I would do the cooking, and no problem. He also told me he did not like to steer but would keep the auto pilot on. With a sinking feeling I started checking everything that would stop the generator from starting, hampered by the very tight installation. The engine room had previously held one genny, now there were two, plus two large banks of batteries and all sorts of electrical paraphernalia. We would need it if the wind went light, as it was expected to do. But nothing I did worked, so we could not charge the batteries and put back all the juice the auto pilot was using.

The next day the wind went to the north and at first we had really good sailing, but then the wind began to fail. Edmund called me up, he had leap frogged us and gone into a marina near Lisbon but we had passed him during the night and now he was leaving port and said he would catch us up before we reached St Vincent. I suspected he would use his engine, not an option for us, so I dug out the small kite, I expect you, dear reader think I am referring to a spinnaker, no such luck, Richard had put on boat two kites, weird things like board kites, I had never seen any like them before. A small one to learn how they work and a big one to fly down wind with. Sadly, there were no instructions. The Dutchman came up and started to help but we could not get the small one to fly. So we tried the big one, after an hour and several near fatalities I put the bloody thing away. The Dutchman went back to bed and I found another old genoa that happily fitted the second luff groove, I hoisted that and dropped the main, suddenly we were doing 5 knots with no effort, Trinity liked the new sail plan.

I called Edmund up on the VHF, after a while he answered, it took a while but he admitted that they had the engine on in an attempt to catch us, but they never did. We reached St Vincent with them still out of sight, I thought it was a very good show on Trinity's behalf. The Dutchman took over and I got my head down after cooking dinner. I always like the Dawn watch, which is a good thing, because just like all fair tide for me seems to mean a 04.00 start, I always seem to pull the graveyard watch. This one was spectacular, first there was a moon, and a pod of dolphins. They were having a great time zooming in and out of the hulls. Then gradually it got light and they went off to look for breakfast. The sunrise was an absolute corker, a flat sea because of the lee of Saint Vincent and a gentle wind that slowly backed until I could put away the other headsail and set the full main. Trinity began to get into her stride. My watch came to an end, so I cooked us some breakfast and went to bed. A few hours later and we were nearly at Portimao, our destination. By now the batteries were almost flat on the 24 volt and 12 volt systems, the starboard generator was working fine but not the port so we only had the starboard engine.

Approaching the marina in Portimao I took over the helm, the Dutchman volunteered to take us in but I told him "It's my responsibility, so if anyone is going to crash Trinity it's going to be me". I knew it would be a tricky manoeuvre, the wind was from the S.E. and after I spoke to the marina I was given a berth that meant docking with the wind on the port bow, there was a bit of tide going past the marina but we got into the shelter of the pontoons and lost that, which entailed a turn to port so that was no problem. But then we needed to turn to starboard, we could not do that without a lot of speed, I tried to get us to blow into the berth allocated to us but there was no way unless we could turn to starboard to get in. I had left the abort route open, (a turn to port and exit the marina) so that's what we did. The Dutchman was not happy and was yapping away in my ear, so I told him to shut up.

I called up the marina and asked for a RIB to help, one duly showed up and I had him lash onto our port side. We went back in and at the right time I had the RIB go gently astern and we slotted in nicely, the Dutchman jumped off the bow and hurt his foot landing on the pontoon. I am not sure why, as the yacht was going in all square, and there were fenders out already.

After the RIB man had gone and we were secure I had to speak with the Dutchman. He beat me to it and said "someday I will teach you how to manoeuvre this boat, but I am glad you had an exit strategy and did not do any damage". It was just too much, so I said "okay so just how would you have done that?" He told me he would have come in with a lot more speed, which was farcical, because the only way of scrubbing the speed off would have been to go hard astern on the starboard engine, which would have made Trinity turn and she would probably would have smashed her rudders off or been pinned across another yachts bow, being blown on by the wind.

I was beginning to dislike the Dutchman intensely. His "charming side" when it slipped revealed a very different character, I just hoped that I could rise above my feelings because if I had to work with him for any length of time I could see things getting ugly. The next day although we were plugged into the shore electricity feed, I could not get the batteries to charge up properly, and when the Dutchman brought some friends aboard who wanted to go for a sail, I disappointed them all by refusing. Later on we met another friend of the Dutchman who was a local and had a car. He drove us over to where Trinity was going to be hauled out. The Dutchman suggested that we hire J (his local friend) I could see the sense to this because J knew the area, could speak English really well and of course had his own wheels, so I agreed. At the boatyard we made the arrangements and agreed a price for Trinity and a container to be hired. Then the Dutchman told the yard manager that he also wanted his own yacht hauled out alongside Trinity.

Back in the car the Dutchman asked me if he could put some of his stuff in the container, I agreed, but I really was beginning to feel uneasy about how things were going. But then he wanted his wife as part of the team to, I told him we would have to ask Richard the owner about that, especially since the Dutchman wanted to pay her an hourly rate of more than twice as much as I would be getting. In fact, I told him that I didn't think the owner would be very pleased to find that the Dutchman's boat was our neighbour, his stuff was in the container and his wife was part of the team. What would happen if he was working on his own yacht and the owner was still paying him? It would look weird.

A couple of days later we hauled out. Again I had to assert my authority and insist on steering Trinity in, slowly. Once again we did not have a problem, but the Dutchman did not like my safe style and made the fact known.

Trinity hauled out in Portimao

Chapter 35

We were hoisted out very professionally and were soon blocked off. Then our container arrived. The Dutchman was miffed because it was not put where he wanted it put. He then went and fetched his tools and we put them in the container and started putting the other stuff in there as well. Our relationship was deteriorating rapidly. Our first boat building job was to measure the yacht after first getting it level. The Dutchman started to get upset, because it quickly became obvious that the yacht was more than a few CMs out of true, he was very embarrassed to admit it to me. He did not like that he had to tell the marine architect that the yacht was not straight. Once we were over that hurdle the marine architect wanted some core samples. I went to start drilling them and the Dutchman went dead weird. He started giving me grief as I began to do it, in the end I told him "the owner of this boat wants samples, I answer to the owner so I am drilling the samples" The Dutchman was in a right strop then, and threw his toys out the pram when I got some dust on him, saying he could not work with someone who risked everybody's health. The fact that a stiff wind was blowing the dust away seemed to have escaped him.

The owner Richard rang me and told me on no account was I to hire on the Dutchman's wife. I agreed with him. The next day I told the Dutchman, "no wife". He started hinting that he might not be able to carry on with the project, and that his original guess at the final price of approximately $60,000 euros had not been for carbon, and with an Architect involved it was going to be much more expensive, closer to $100,000 euros. I was beginning to hope that Richard, when he heard that might ask me to take Trinity back to the U.K.

Helen came to visit. It was good to see her. I did not say anything about the Dutchman but in about two seconds flat she told me she did not like him at all. She was there when we started to construct the tent. We needed a windproof/ rain proof shelter that would stand up to the quite strong winds. The Dutchman had designed it and we had worked out the materials we needed. It was hellishly expensive, but Richard was okay with paying for it. So the wood was ordered, which they would deliver. J took me and the Dutchman to get the plastic sheet we needed. In the shop they had the right stuff, really strong plastic, but only in dark green. We could not wait for them to get it in white, so green it was. Several boxes of screws and builders foam later and we were ready to roll. No wood, as it had not been delivered yet. I asked J to chase it up, which he did. But still the wood did not show up. The next day I called them and asked to speak to someone who could talk English, a manager was put on " Hi we are waiting for our wood" I said, " yes it will be there this afternoon" he said, " yes , we were told that yesterday, if it is not here by 4pm the order is cancelled". J and the Dutchman looked at me "you cannot talk to people like that in this country" the Dutchman said. I told him I could and left it at that. In truth I was getting really fed up of having to tip toe around so as not to hurt people's feelings. I was used to working with men who were a bit more resilient.

The wood arrived at ten minutes past 4 and we stowed it in the container. The next day we finally got to work. However, my hopes for an easier time were well and truly dashed a couple of days later.

We did not start early, it was usually 09.30 before everyone was at the boat. I like to start with a cup of tea and a short discussion about what was going to be done each day. This particular day people were late and then wanted tea and biscuit by then it was

10.30, and I threw my toys out the pram and said in a loud voice "for F...ks sake can we please start now, or nothing will get done today." The Dutchman looked at me like I was from another planet, and put his cup down to start work. All day he was a seething mass of unexpressed resentment working like a man possessed. He worked with J and I just did as much as I could, keeping up with him to see how long he could keep the pace. Finally, the light had gone I had started making mistakes out of tiredness. We were working with torches when J started up the circular saw to cut a bit of wood. I said "right that's enough, someone is going to get hurt, call it a day" and I started to put stuff away. The atmosphere was so thick you could have cut it with a knife. They went. And I could look forward to another fun filled day tomorrow.

More of this nonsense followed. If I made a mistake measuring something the Dutchman would make a big thing of it, in the end he said in a very patronising way "we are going to get you fetching things as J is better at the construction work than you" I said "but it's okay if I keep making the tea is it?" My sarcasm was not lost on him, we both knew what was going on. He wanted me gone, the reason was very obvious. The stupid thing was I did not want even to be there. I felt very much like a fish out of water, but the more he tried to get me to go the more I wanted to stay. I have always had a stubborn streak, and I have always hated being bullied, and this was all this was. As well as this the situation was in many ways similar to what had happened recently at Thurrock Yacht Club. I realised that for my own wellbeing I had to make a stand this time no matter what it cost me.

Helen went back to the U.K. and I went too as the Dutchman had to take a week or so off, so we were going to be a bit quite. I received and email from the owner with an attached e mail from the

Dutchman accusing me of all kinds of scurrilous behaviour, he asked me what I thought of it. I told him I thought it was nonsense. He asked me to answer it. I did so, refuting the charges and attempting to make peace. However, my email was sent back with a torrent of abuse attached. I told the owner I had no intention of rising to the bait. It looked like we had no boat builder on the team anymore. The owner's take on the situation was interesting he said "He wants more power, he wants you out of the way, I do not trust him and I will not go ahead without you there" This was all very flattering, by also very scary. I was hopeful of finding someone else who could do the work, so I returned to Portugal a few days later.

Scarcely had I arrived back on the boat when my phone went it was the Dutchman being oily and charming again, "Hi Max, I have been let down on a place to stow the carbon and epoxy resin I have brought back from Holland can I put it in the container?" Alarm bells rang loudly in my head, we had not agreed a price for the carbon and epoxy, so if I let him put it in the container he could argue that I had accepted delivery, as well as that this man had been doing his level best to get me fired a few days ago, I was not inclined to do him a favour and did not trust him an inch "no" I said. "In that case I take my tools away" he declared, with no charm at all.

In the morning he arrived at the boatyard with J, and he took his tools away. The next day he was back all smiles. He took me in his new Land Rover that he had bought in Holland to see the house he had rented. It was close by, and it had a spare top floor flat he told me I could rent it off him if I wanted... It also had a huge garage where he could mould the Ama parts. We went across the road for a beer. He was being very friendly. He wanted back on the team, and we could not really do the work without him, he said. His kids and wife would be arriving soon and he had already paid for the kid's private education in the International school. Obviously all the past upsets had been a misunderstanding. He did have a point. I had never been involved with moulding Carbon parts or doing any large boat building before, so hoping that at last he had learnt his lesson I agreed to him coming back.

Richard was not impressed, "if he is coming back I want a contract signed by him stating exactly what he is going to do for us". The next day the Dutchman showed up, all smiles, over coffee on board of Trinity, I broached the subject of a contract, he reared up and started shouting at me, lapsing into Dutch and all but frothing that the mouth. I was very glad when he had gone. J was there and he worked the rest of the day, helping me working on the shelter, but he was very quiet. J showed up the next day for work, but there was obviously something on his mind, and in the afternoon he told me he was going to work with the Dutchman because he was his friend, I paid him off and that was that.

Chapter 36

The boatyard was a big area, and a lot of the yachts that had hauled out over winter were also Dutch. I found I had become a bit of a pariah and I was generally ignored by most of them. However, a German couple (Wulf and Steffi) aboard a catamaran would still talk to me and we became good friends. I also discovered the wonderful Algarve beaches during the Sundays I always took off. My favourite beach was only accessible by climbing down a crumbly cliff, the last 10 meters was managed by the aid of a rope that was tied to some iron stakes deeply imbedded in the limestone fossil filled cliff. This beach was mostly empty and I enjoyed soaking up the sun and swimming in the crystal clear water without having to wear a swimming costume. This beach was to become my sanctuary from the stress of the Trinity project the pristine ocean and beach never failing to bring things back into perspective even in the darkest times.

One of the few problems with being based in Portugal is that the wines and Ports are really good and very cheap, I wanted to maintain a good standard of physical fitness, and it would have been all too easy to go for a drink at the end of a day or during the week end. I knew at all costs I had to stay away from the bars and other yacht people who drank a lot. So even when later people became friendlier around me I still had to keep my distance. Many of the people around me were retired and not on a work schedule, not my situation at all.

I hit the phones the next day - it was not encouraging, Carbon fibre specialists were few and far between in Portugal. In fact, the closest I got was a British shipwright who I tracked down who told me of a place that would mould me two Amas if I could get the old ones to them, It would be a major job to cut the old ones off, and then reattach the new ones. Along with the transport problems of moving two 14 meter parts across Portugal, the price was astronomical - approx. 100,000 euros each.

Finally, I called Clive - a shipwright friend of mine in the U.K. I asked if he knew anyone who could help me. Wonder of wonders he did! He gave me the contact details of Paul Wells, who had been building and rebuilding yachts including many multihulls for years, using all kinds of exotic materials. He even had a company that built carbon masts. He also used to live in Portugal not far from where we were.

I called him straight away, he answered and asked me to send him pictures and more details. Something about his voice told me instantly I could trust him. I sent him an e mail and did not beat about the bush - I told him the whole sorry story and sent photos.

While I was waiting for an answer I got on with stripping the boat of its sea going gear. The sails had to be taken off, the dagger boards removed and so on. All the gear was heavy and at one point I saw the Dutchman and J watching me from the road, I ignored them and got on with the job. An English man came up to me and started to chat. He asked me what I was doing. I was a bit wary because I had seen him in the company of the Dutchman before, but I showed him around and said I was looking for some help. He said he was looking for some work and so he joined the team.

Paul arranged to visit us the next week to have a look at the job. The owner had asked me what tools I needed. I gave him a wish list - all the best Festool gear, not expecting to get half of it. To my amazement he had bought everything and he asked if Paul would bring it. I asked Paul who said "I want to see the owner in London anyway, if it's not too much stuff I will pick it up from him". But fate intervened in the form of flooding in the S.W. of the U.K. Paul was helping his friends dry their house out until the last minute and then went to Gatwick. I told the owner who said he would take the tools to Paul.

Richard finally arrived at the airport 10 minutes before the gates closed with 5 very heavy holdalls! He gave them to Paul and a £50 note and said "that should cover it" Paul said "I think it's going to be more than that, you had better go and talk to them." The final bill for extra hold luggage was an eye watering £470.

I had booked Paul into a cheap but nice hotel not far from the yard. When he arrived that evening, I met him and helped him up to his room with the holdalls. I was astonished at their weight and could but wonder how Richard had managed on all the underground trains and stairs to get them to the airport. I suggested that we should eat out around the corner. Over dinner Paul told me the story of how he has almost missed the plane waiting for the bags, then he asked me what the owner did for a living as this must be costing him a fortune. "It's okay he can afford it, he's an arms dealer" I told him. Paul digested this and his face went white, because obviously he had not had time to look in the really heavy bags….! I said "only kidding, he is into I.T. security! It was a good joke and broke the ice. By the end of the evening I was very sure that Paul was the man who was going to sort the whole thing out and for the first time in a long time things were starting to look up, I couldn't wait for the next day.

Paul arrived early, he said he had been up since 06.30, walking about and enjoying coffee on the sea front. As soon as M arrived Paul dropped his bombshell "the only way we are going to know what is really going on is to cut off the stern of an Ama, the stern starboard one looks easiest". I got out the cutting tools and we started work. It took a couple of days, but finally the 6 metre part was lowered onto the floor. Several things became immediately apparent; 1, the part was impossibly heavy, the epoxy and glass applied to keep the hull together when the dagger boards and new rudders were fitted, was in some parts 25mm thick! 2, the hull had several layers and was breaking up. A large amount of the original outer glass and epoxy had not stuck to the plywood and peeled off like wet wall paper. Even the polystyrene had been stuck to the inner plywood with what looked to be some kind of floor adhesive, and that was also coming apart. I remembered the test I had done on the deck board, it had not been built like the hull was, at least the deck board's parts stayed together. Paul said "I have never ever seen anything like this, how on earth did the builder ever think this was going to hold up". Suddenly the Dutchman's weird behaviour became a bit more understandable, but not forgivable. I had pushed Trinity hard in the Bay thinking she was strong, in reality she could have broken up at any point. Partly my own stupidity in not believing the Architect, assuming the hull was built the same as the engine room deck board, and trusting the Dutchman. Paul told me not to worry, it could all be fixed. I was very interested to learn how.

Chapter 37

Over coffee he outlined a plan. We would use the part we had cut off to make a plug and cast a shape from it in Carbon Fibre with a high density foam core. This shape would then be 30mm too big (because that was the thickness of the core) so we would then cut the shape in two, fit it and mark and cut where the middle was and eventually arrive at a new shape that would fit into the hull. Then we would remove all the horrid falling to bits' rubbish that was what the old hull was made of, except for the inner skin. We would then make all good with carbon fibre and high density core until we had a strong light hull again, after which we would use the plugs to make shapes for the other Ama hull and do the same. We also had to call Richard the owner and tell him it was not worth just renewing the underwater parts of the Amas. 90% of the hulls had to be rebuilt but we could get away with not doing the deck. Richard was not surprised - he said delamination had been reported in the surveys he had commissioned. He told us to go ahead and fix the hulls. I mentioned it might be better to build a new boat, but he was adamant that he wanted just wanted "Trinity" fixed properly this time.

To do this we needed to learn some stuff - the techniques of "Carbon Vacuum bagging" and how to make the parts we cut off into plugs. M who had made a couple of yachts in the past from moulds was very sceptical of this idea, he wanted to make a mould. Paul explained it would take a lot of extra time to make a mould, not to mention material, and it was not needed. Paul made a list of stuff we required and we set to finding it. We also had to change the shape a bit, as the marine architect wanted a fuller more buoyant shape and 1.5 meters longer at the stern. M drove us 60 kilometres to Oliho to the only shop that sold fiberglass materials. Paul who supply's that kind of thing in the U.K. could hardly believe the prices; "we will get what we need here today, but I am going to have to supply you from the U.K. this is approx. 4x what we charge". That day we bought Foam (for shaping) polyester resin, mixing buckets, rollers thermometers, and chopped strand matt.

The next day we started making the plug. We used the part of the stern we had cut off. Turning it upside down and getting it level gave us a starting point. We had a plan from the architect we worked out at what point the lines started to become fuller, and stuck foam from there backwards. Until we came to the stern, then we extended it with sheets of foam eventually we arrived at the basic form we wanted. Then we shaped it and covered it in chopped strand matt and polyester resin. Over this we laid on car body filler, this was then sanded down with long boards that had coarse sandpaper attached. Over a few days one side of the new shape appeared, but then Paul had to go back. He left us with a long job list and told us he would be back in a couple of months. M and I got stuck in - there was lots to get on with.

I had not seen the Dutchman for a while and I hoped he had gone, but it was not to be. One day I saw his own trimaran heading towards the haul out place, and his boat was brought into a spot only 50 metres from where we were. I resolved to ignore him, and did my best to.

I received a call from Edmund out of the blue. He was taking a big Halberg Rassy to the Caribbean. He was stormbound in Lisbon and as the weather looked foul for a few days he would like to visit. He arrived by train and It was extremely good to see him. As we made our way back to the tri, we stopped at several bars on the way.

There was much to talk about and by the time we were on the final stretch our bladders were very full, I suggested we relive them on an old classic yacht's keel. It was the perfect place because the yacht had once been owned by Adolf Hitler. Edmund agreed. Our wee must have been pretty potent, because that old wooden yacht sunk at her moorings a few months after being launched.

The following morning, I noted that Edmund's annoying ability to not have hangovers was still evident, as my head was a bit thick. The wind and rain prevented any work from happening so Edmund had a good tour of the yacht and the work that needed doing. I explained all the problems I had been having, he suggested that should anyone ask who he was then we could say he was the owner's Lawyer and that should shake the Dutchman up! Over the next couple of days, we had a great time - it was just so good to be able to talk to someone of Edmund's experience. I was very sorry to wave him good bye, and very jealous of the trip he had before him.

Christmas came and I went back for a couple of weeks - it was good to see everybody and to get away from the work. I saw poor Gloria, she was okay but green stuff was growing all over her deck. Helen and I had a huge row, and I went and stayed on Gloria for a few days. I then had to go and see the owner on New Year's Eve. On the way back I had a call from Helen who was crying, her cat was very ill and had to go to the vet. I knew that probably the cat would not be coming back home so I volunteered to go with her.

It was a desperately sad affair. The cat (Jeff) was very old and had survived several close calls with the vet and his hypodermic. Helen had always said that as long as Jeff was still enjoying life she would not have her put down. Sadly, the poor thing could hardly eat anymore. I think she knew what was on the cards because she crept out into the garden as we got the cat box ready, and I had to go and find her. At the vets I was allowed to stroke her and say goodbye as he put the needle in, she gave me a very reproachful look and closed her eyes. Mine and Helen's filled with tears. We took her into the park next to Helen's house and buried her by her favourite path, just as fireworks started to mark the New Year. Our quarrel was forgotten and I stayed with Helen over the next few days and tried to make up for the time we had wasted until it was time to go back to Portugal. I was very sad to go.

I was not having a lot of fun still. I found M difficult to work with, and I was still persona non grata with most of the live a board's in the yard. I wanted to chuck it all in and go sailing, but I knew that if I gave up this project it would stick to me always. The only way out was to see it through.

We finished the plug making part on the stern section. While we waited for Paul to finish what he was doing, M and I cut the bow section off. The plug-making began on that part. It was not a smooth operation. For one thing we had happened to pick the wettest winter for 40 years to work in. Although our shelter was up it was not 100% water proof, nowhere near, really. Rain would bring us to a standstill. The other was supplies of car body filler. We were going through boxes of it. The only place we could find that sold it in bulk was near Faro, 55 kilometres away. M had the car and would take most of the day going and coming back from there, so that it was only 30 minutes from knocking time and not worth getting into anything else. Another source of friction was the shape, the owner wanted "Dreadnought" bows, (sloping backwards). The architect said it was not possible and drew plumb (straight up and down) bows, I disliked either option on the grounds of aesthetics, because we would not be able to change the shape of the main hull's bow. It would look really odd with one traditional bow and the Ama's with something that did not have the same shape. I found an earlier plan that the owner had drawn of a more traditional bow that fitted in with the main hull's bow. So I made that.

Our supplies of Carbon Fibre and Ampreg 21 epoxy resin finally showed up and I carefully put them away. Paul was not far behind them, it was very good to see him. Helen also paid us a visit. I hired a car and rented a chalet overlooking the hills, hoping she would stay. We were incredibly busy and I did not have much time with her. We had to (among other things) build a vacuum pump. The owner wanted to buy one from America, but it was hellishly expensive at £4000. Paul bought the basic pump for £700 and I got the local welder to mount it onto an old gas cylinder with 4 outlets with ball valves. Some wheels, a handle and some hose completed the affair. Another piece of equipment we needed was a diesel blower heater. Helen tracked one down on the internet and we rushed off to buy it in the car.

Finally, everything was in place for us to make our first bit of carbon fibre sandwich. It was complicated - we first placed sealing tape around the outside edges of the plug. Then we coated the surface of the plug with resin. Next we laid "peel ply" (a sort of nylon sheet) onto this resin and carefully rolled the air out, Then, this was coated with more resin. On top of this we laid a laminate of carbon, again removing the air so it laid flat and un-creased. Another coat of resin and another laminate, more resin and a last laminate. More resin and rolling. Finally, when all the air was out we put on another layer of peel ply. Then over this was laid a sheet of "bleed film" (thin plastic with lots of little holes). Over this we placed a sheet of "breather blanket" that would let the air flow and soak up any excess resin. Finally we could put the bag on and make it air tight. This was easier said than done because resin had dripped over the sealing rubber in some places, and it would not stick. Using acetone, we cleaned it until we could get a seal. We could not wear gloves when we handled the sealing tape because it stuck to them, so it was simply impossible not to get epoxy resin on our skin at times. As soon as we could we had to get this off our skin, first with acetone and then with warm soapy water, and all the time the clock was ticking.

Two hoses had been put in from the pump and we switched it on. After much chasing of hissing noises, we finally achieved an airtight seal. Then we turned it off and consulted our scales and the clock. You see, if the vacuum is turned on too early it sucks all the resin out. So we had to work out with the temperature and the time of the first mix of resin to the time of the last mix of resin, when we could start the vacuum. The joker in the pack with this was that as we were soon to learn, the air temperature and that of the carbon on the plug could quite often be very different, and we had to watch out for that all the while. At the appropriate moment, we turned on the pump. Once it was established we had a good vacuum, we rolled in a heating up tent I had made of plastic over a framework of wooded battens. It was relatively light but long enough to house the whole part and the diesel heater. When we fired up the heater we could get the temperature up to 50 c which allowed the epoxy to cure much faster.

Of course, there was always a risk of fire - the epoxy, acetone, plastic, wooden battens were all highly combustible and we had to always be on our guard. We could never leave the machines going by themselves, just in case.

3 hours later it had cured and everything could be turned off. That was the first performance, and we only made one panel, onto that we next had to bond high density foam core, again under vacuum. That was then shaped with long sanding-boards and filled. Then to that we added another 3 laminates of carbon fibre. 3 days and 32 separate actions to make one part. I realised there was an awful lot of work to be done. It even took us hours to clean up after each vacuuming session.

Paul was a wonderful teacher - he never lost his temper and was always in a good mood. He answered any questions as if they were sensible, and kept his patience even if they were daft. He kept us going over and over the process until we began to get it and never went on until he was sure we understood everything.

The days passed too quickly, and Helen had to go home. I was down about that when the Dutchman made an appearance again. He and J were working on his boat, unfortunately I had to walk past, he said something that I just ignored and carried on to throw some rubbish away at the skip. On the way back he again had a dig, something about finding someone else to do the work, I disregarded this too. Then he called me a coward, and the red mist descended. I threw the big bucket I had down and walked up to him and asked why he thought I was a coward he came up with some nonsense about an email I sent to him, that he had sent to his wife! I told him what I thought of him, his rubbish boat building and his slimy back stabbing manner. I told him that it was time to settle things, and he could have first punch. He didn't want to know, but I was steaming by then and shouting all kinds of profanity at him, trying to kick it off. He had never seen me really angry before and I think because of his size he was not used to people squaring up to him. I walked away quite glad that it had not come to violence because he is quite a big lump, but I really did fancy a go at adjusting that long thin nose of his!

Sadly a few of the live a board's were about one who had a small kid with them, they quite rightly were not very happy with me. I went over and apologised some days later. Paul told me to calm it down and not start trouble, and that the Dutchman was trying to wind me up, which he probably was.

The days flew past, we were learning fast and working hard. M had bought a new car and was not up to fetching the things we needed in it so I fitted a rack to my bike and I did all the go getting. It was very pleasant - most of the time the weather was very mild and the flat terrain made cycling a dream. Sometimes however, it rained hard and we could not work. On one such day I called M and told him not to bother as the site was flooded. Paul showed up as usual and took the opportunity to go over the work we had to do, and as the sun came out we went for a walk. There was plenty to discuss about the job and the walk turned into a bit of a hike. We were in Alvore before we turned around. Alvore is about 8 kilometres west of us. The cliff walks there are very dramatic. On the way back we went by the marina and I saw some Dutch people I had met before. Unfortunately, they are good friends of the Dutchman, but I was surprised when the lady called me over and offered us coffee. We had a good conversation, both of them had worked extensively with epoxy and they enjoyed talking to Paul. Towards the end the lady said "but the work you are doing, is it really necessary? After all Trinity was built beautifully". Paul explained that Trinity was falling apart, but I could see they did not really believe us. I did not want to start slagging the Dutchman down to them, so we left it at that and left. However, I now had an idea of how to handle the Dutchman once and for all.

A few days later after we had finished making the first complete part M hit us with a bombshell, first of all he asked for his pay on Friday morning. I paid him thinking he had a bill to settle. Come knocking off time he announced that that had been his last day and he would not be in on Monday. I thought it was a joke, but no he was quitting. I asked him "why" and he unbuttoned his top pocket and produced a list, he started reading it, most of it was to do with my short comings as a manager. I did start to try and talk him out of leaving, but I suddenly I had enough and told him to "just piss off then", which he did. From my way of thinking the worst insult you can give an employer is to walk off the job without notice, it means that you don't care about any problem your absence is going to cause, it just a blatant insult. As he walked off I saw the Dutchman and his wife, on their boat, with grins as wide as any Cheshire cat's, his wife even waved, It seemed quite apparent that they knew M was leaving and that he had been talking to them.

Paul was less than amused. And when I told Richard the owner, he was really unhappy. "Offer him more money" he said, which was funny because M was already getting paid more than me on an hourly rate. So I said "under no circumstances." I knew I would never be able to work with him again. A replacement was needed quickly but luckily I had spotted someone who had good connections who I thought could help. Alberto was a retired university lecturer, and something of a local hero. His father had been jailed in the 1970s for political reasons, and then to hurt him more, so had the young Alberto. In 1974 there had been a bloodless revolution and all those who had been visibly against the old regime became rightly very popular. Alberto, who owned a Catana Catamaran that he was fixing up so he could sail around the world with his son, worked hard and seemed like a decent kind of man - sane and calm. He seemed to know everyone and was well liked. I went over and had a word. I told him that I needed someone to help us, and that he would need to be able to speak good English as my Portuguese was rubbish. He said to leave it with him as he had someone who might be able to help.

Chapter 38

A couple of days later he sent a guy to see us, his name was Wido. Although he had lived for 30 years in Portugal he was Dutch! He had never worked on boats before but had spent many years fitting kitchens. Tall and broad shouldered he was the best worker I had ever met. He always showed up early, had to be told to go home, he had a great sense of humour and never complained. Above all of this though, was his standard of work. He would never leave a job unless he was happy with it. His skills as a kitchen fitter directly transferred to the work we were doing. Paul was very pleased, as was the owner.

Fairly soon we had at last finished with the bow plug, having made all four panels from it. I could now put my plan into action to get the Dutchman off my back. Wido and I dragged the bow section outside and put it on display alongside our shelter, turning the cut part towards the Dutchman's yacht. Everyone could then see the delamination and the fact that the hull was made of very substandard material. From our conversation with his friends I knew the tale he had been spinning but with the evidence of the sub-standard materials used and the result on display, anyone could see what had really happened. As he was attempting to find more boatbuilding work in the area, this display was very damaging to his reputation, It did not give me any pleasure to do this - I would rather have been friends, but all the time he was about I knew he would be attempting to get rid of me some way or another so, this had to be done. It worked and we saw less and less of him, until one day his Trimaran was craned back in the water and he went off to Croatia.

Like I said, I would rather have been friends. A lot of the work on Trinity that he had done was awesome, and I really liked the design inside and the way the space had been used. And the way Trinity sailed, planted and very fast. There was a lot very good about Trinity and I think that was why Richard wanted to throw money at her and turn her into the yacht she could be. It was the first boat the Dutchman built I think - he was young and maybe a bit too ambitious. I would not have had the nerve to have started that project when I was his age. Where she fell down was the cheap materials she had been constructed from and the fact that the Epoxy had not bonded the two outer glass cloth laminates to the plywood, I don't know why this happened, but it could have had dire consequences. The other major problem was windward ability. I sailed her before she had the dagger boards fitted and with only stub keels and a draft of about 1 meter, as you would expect, she made excessive lee way. Yes, just like the Lagoon I sailed, you could get her to point up, but a causal glance at the chart plotter revealed the true story. Just like any other sailing craft, Trinity had to have something in the water to get a grip, the dagger boards worked really well to solve this problem, but it was a shame the engineering done to fit them was so appalling.

Paul had to go back before we put the first bow on properly, but he had showed us how to do it, and soon it was up there in all its carbon fibre glory. The work was hard but very satisfying; each day there was something to show for our efforts.

Edmund called me. He was back from quite an exciting trip taking the Halberg Rassy to the Caribbean. All had gone very well until 1000 miles away from Barbados, when while Edmund was below fixing the evening meal, the owner who had been trying to repair the wind generator, fell overboard. The wind was blowing about a force 7, the light was starting to go and of course the yacht was set up for downwind sailing. Somehow Edmund managed the whole situation so well that the (almost non-swimming) owner was back on board dripping onto the cockpit sole within 20 minutes. That's a situation that has always been a nightmare of mine and probably most skippers, which is why good skippers like Edmund ceaselessly practice the "Man overboard drill". He also suggested that he come over for a few days the next month or so. I looked forward to seeing him.

Meanwhile the bow was on and grafted in so we started work on the stern, moulding up the panels and getting one ready for fitting. About a month later I had another message from Edmund, he was ill. The doctors though it was pneumonia. Then another message came in, poor Edmund had cancer. I immediately went back to the U.K. to see him at an Oxford hospital. His sense of humour was still evident and he liked the whisky I brought him. His daughter Arabella and his Wife Teresa were also there. Although he obviously had trouble breathing he seemed quite hopeful of making a recovery and of starting chemo soon. There was not much I could do - I felt totally useless. Anything that came out of my mouth just seemed banal or ridiculous. After a while I left and drove Helen's car back home. I was only back for a week, and I was not very good company.

One of the things I missed most about being away from home was walking "Boss" Helen's son's staffie. He is a lovely dog, all muscle and looks fearsome, but he is such a softy that if another dog picks on him he runs home. This May Day of spring's promise, Helen and I took Boss for a walk in the ancient woodlands near her house. It was idyllic, with the woodland waking up after winter, but on the path basking in the warm sunlight, I spotted an Adder. Before I could stop him Boss ran over it. It struck so fast I did not even see it move, and I thought the dog had gotten away with it. Helen and I took photos of the snake as he glided off into the undergrowth, happy to have seen such a beautiful creature. Then after about five minutes, Boss fell over and we realised he had been bitten after all. I asked Helen to go and get her car and drive it to the entrance of the woods, and I started to run after her carrying Boss, (who weights a ton). Normally he won't let anyone pick him up, but this day he just lay there. I ran and fast walked the mile or so, my arms and shoulders on fire. We reached the entrance just as Helen appeared with the car and I put Boss on the back seat for the short journey to the vets. There the vet was sceptical of a snake bite, until we showed her the photos, but even then she was reluctant to administer anti venom until later Boss started to show signs of obvious distress. The fact was we had reached the vet in such a short amount of time the symptoms had not really begun to show, so happily he made a complete recovery.

Returning back in Portugal the work carried on, but then I had another message from Edmund asking if I could come and see him again. I did, but I could not get away for a few days, I arrived on the 7th of May, and sent a text message to him. On The 8th of May there was a reply, but from Arabella his daughter, telling me that Edmund had passed on that morning. I was completely and utterly gutted. I can only imagine how his wife Teresa and his family felt.

I stayed for the funeral, and Helen came with me. The ceremony took place in a beautiful small very old church in an Oxford village near where Arabella has her Riding school and Stud farm. The service was simple and the last song was very appropriate, it was the Kinks "sailing on sunny afternoon".

My abiding memory of Edmund in happier times

Chapter 39

Returning once more to Portugal, I bought a sea Kayak. The evenings were getting nice and I started going for a paddle at the end of the day and sometimes in the morning. It was good to get afloat again. I also spent my Sundays on the beach if the tide was good, never tiring of its beauty. I also found a "clothing optional" resort that was on my door step, for 15 euros I bought a year's membership that entitled me to use the pool, tennis court and extensive library. This place was called "Quinta da Horta, and it was just a really relaxing environment with small cottages guests could stay in. The manager Ted was really easy going and his wife Val very friendly. It was started many years ago as a retreat for artists, and had gradually evolved into a holiday place. Sometimes I would be invited to eat there in the evening. It was a very quiet and calm space something I desperately needed then. Helen went mental when she found out, but after I finally convinced her that it was not a den of inequity she calmed down a bit.

The work progressed and we approached the moment when both ends of the starboard Ama where rebuilt, but we needed Paul back to show us how to do the middle part. He showed up and started to work his magic. I was expecting to be able to use the old Dagger board housing as they looked a bit heavy but well built. Paul convinced me otherwise. Although vast amounts of materials had been used (at huge cost to the owner) nothing had been done right. For example, the carbon dagger boards were housed in eight white nylon type blocks, each block weighted 3.5 kilos. Each block was bolted in only at the ends, when the dagger board was put under pressure the blocks deflected and the whole stress was put on a thin area where a shelf was, almost guaranteed to snap the dagger board on that stress line. It all had to be cut out and replaced and the job done properly.

There was a lot to be done and we got on with it, and although we became a very good team, there was some problems. I went after the old dagger board housing with a 9-inch angle grinder fitted with a diamond cutting disc. This monster is a nasty bit of kit in a confined space, lots of noise and if the disc catches up it's hard to stop it going out of control, it's also heavy dusty, hot work. The only way I can do jobs like that is aggressively. I ripped into it, we had a big hole cut into the side and I threw the first big nylon block through it. Before I did that I shouted "Below" meaning "get from below" so people would know to stay out the way. Wido shouted back "yes" so I threw the next one and it hit Wido who thought I was calling him, really hard in the hand. Talk about the law of unforeseen consequences - who would have thought Wido's parents would almost get him killed by naming him with something that sounds like "Below"!!

Later that afternoon (which was a Saturday) Nick next door happened to hold a BBQ. We were invited, and that night we all drank too much wine. Poor Wido arrived home to be met by his wife at 02.00 the next morning with his hand still swollen and bleeding, not being able to talk very well he was sent to bed to sleep it off. I woke up on Sunday morning with a bad head. Paul though it hilarious. I suggested going to the Quinta da Horta (the clothing optional place) for a quite swim in the pool followed by some time on a lounger in the sun - nothing too exerting. Paul agreed if he could keep his shorts on, which of course he could. I wanted him to see the place anyway so he could be a witness that there was nothing at all sleazy about it. On arrival I took the key from its hiding place and let us in, moving to the pool area I disrobed, had a shower and joined the people in the pool. My head was still like it was filled with cotton wool, otherwise I might have noticed something was amiss. As it was I emerged from the pool and found a lounger to stretch out on in the hot sunshine. Ted the manager found me there some little time later, he said "Max, you know this place is clothing optional?" "Yes Ted" I replied, "well not this week, it's been booked by a yoga club" Paul still wearing his shorts was doubled over laughing, I began to notice the other people, and yes they all had swimming costumes on - well the ones that had not left in fury!

The days passed quite pleasantly. Early in the morning I would either ride my mountain bike up to the cliffs, climb down the rope, running down across the course sandy beach before plunging into the beautiful turquoise sea that was a perfect temperature. I would swim for 15 minutes East along the coast to the next beach then either run back across the sand or swim back. When I started taking a snorkel and mask with me I saw the fish life and gradually became almost on first name terms with them. After climbing back up the cliff I would ride my bike to the village shop to get fresh bread and eggs. About twice a week I would go for a paddle in my kayak to see what yachts were at anchor in the bay – and all of this before breakfast. The work started at 09.00 and we would put in a good morning's graft before I started up the BBQ. Our lunch was usually pork, chicken or sausages, with kebabs of red, green peppers and tomatoes. We even had a dog - well sort of. She belonged to Jeff and Marin who had a catamaran called "Miss Poe". Their dog "Flora" would show up when she smelt the BBQ. She was very good natured and fooled us completely into trusting her. On the one time both Wido and I were called away for a few minutes she got the lot! Never trust a dog around a BBQ. We would work until about 17.00. I usually made dinner and Paul and I would talk for a bit mostly about the job before I had to go and get my head down. Sometimes Paul took me out for dinner, as he was not into cooking.

The complicated dagger board housing was made from a mould Paul and Wido built - it was a quarter of the weight of the old one and far stronger, but before Paul could fit it his time was up and he had to go back. He left instructions for its fitting and Wido and I managed to get it in and lined up. I took no chances and we manhandled the dagger board itself up on top and with the help of the main boom, lowered it into its slot, so I could be absolutely sure it was straight. When we finally got it in the correct position we started bonding the housing in so it would never move again. Once it was all cured off we tried lowering and hauling up the board with its own lifting equipment, and it was surprisingly easy and smooth.

The rebuild of Trinity using carbon fibre sandwich construction.
Wido hard at work!

Chapter 40

The summer became hotter, quite often both Wido and I could only work in shorts and flipflops, and still be streaming with sweat - and that was in the shade! We had to be very careful when we mixed up resin as the amount of time we could use it could be very brief. One time Wido was doing some filling, I mixed up a small pot of filler, gave it to him, he used one gob of it, went back for another bit and it had already started to set and the pot was smoking. But we managed to keep going, mostly by setting everything up so we did the laminating early in the morning when it was a bit cooler. At the end of the day I quite often went back to the beach and plunged into the clean salty sea to wash the dust and sweat out of my hair and off of my skin.

A large ketch called "Elly Grey" was brought into the yard, it had wooden masts and a gaff rig. The hull was the most wonderful shape, I was not surprised to find it had been built by Martin Heard of Heard yacht fame. I still think the Heard 23 one of the most perfectly shaped boats I had ever seen. I managed to get a look around her and realised I was looking at my dream yacht, along with a small pilot house, big bronze deck wear, a Jacuzzi in the counter stern she had a Gardiner 6LX engine. I was smitten! The owner (Vail Clewly) cut the bow sprit off 10 foot shorter. He said it did not need to be that big. But then the forestay fitting had to be raised up the mast so the stay would be the right tension. After a while of talking to Vail he asked me if I would do some work up the mizzen mast. After work one evening I went up there and did the work. I have good power to weight ratio, so that kind of thing is easy for me. He was so impressed he asked me to sort out the main mast. There were several jobs that needed doing and after working on Trinity most nights Wido and I would get busy on Elly Grey. Vail insisted on cooking for us, and he was a brilliant cook. However, the meals were all hot and in the blistering heat even in the evening they were often hard to consume! His wife came over, a lovely Thai lady (Pen) who ran a restaurant in Falmouth. She cooked a meal for us one night, it was probably the best Thai meal I have ever eaten. Fortunately, with all the cycling, swimming, kayaking and mast climbing I did not get fat.

The Trimaran was slowly evolving into a carbon fibre sailing machine. When we first started people used to come in and laugh, now when we had visitors they were mostly very impressed. It would have been hard not have been. The carbon was very light but incredibly strong, and visually of huge impact. Wido and I were getting more and more used to handling it, and much quicker at getting it on and the airtight bag sealed.

In August I had to go home to move my own boat "Gloria" to a yard that would take her out of the water. I arrived on the 7th, got her running on the 8th and we left on the 10th. "We" being myself and Dave (pigtail) the Bosun at Thurrock Yacht Club. It was not without incident. Poor Gloria was silted into her berth, and we were late getting out. We had 10 minutes of making tide when we finally left, it was not enough for that ditch (which the upper reaches of the crouch without any traffic has become) and we slid gracefully to a halt half a mile down the river. I laid out the anchors at low water and Dave dug a trench and at half an hour before H.W. we got off, this time making Brandy Hole without any more grief. There Justin promised to get her out as soon as the tide became high enough and there was a trailer available.

Chapter 41

I had a few days with Helen then went back to Portugal and work. Wulf and Steffi on the catamaran Aqua vite were often in the anchorage and I would always stop for a coffee or beer and a chat. They told me about a man they had met who had built a catamaran on the banks of the Gambian river - apparently he was quite a character. A few days later I had the chance to find out for myself as he showed up with his fine vessel next to the boatyard. He was a tall wiry German/Swiss who went by the name of "Hans" and had been brought up on an old Chinese Junk by his father and mother. His father had served a full term in the French Foreign Legion, and Hans had such tales to tell! I went to have dinner with Wulf and Steffi on the Catamaran he had built. It was made of Mahogany planks. Han's knew what he wanted and by using Google Earth he found a traditional boat building area on the banks of the Gambian river. He had then flown there with a big holdall of good quality stainless steel bolts, some money, and a model of the boat he wanted. He then found the man, an old well-seasoned shipwright who during his long and productive career had not only built many fine vessels but had fathered seven sons and passed to them his shipwright skills. Between them they could bring Han's dream into reality. The next steps were to reach a deal, then buy the mahogany trees, get them transported to the beach, turn them into planks, build the two hulls, plank up the bridge deck, step a mast and fix the rudders. It took 3 months.

When she was finished he called her "Ontong Java" and she was one of the most beautiful boats I ever saw.

Hans is an artist - not one of those who puts on airs and courts admiration, but one of those who cannot do even the simplest tasks without imbuing it with some aesthetic magic. It was so with his boat, Ontong. She was a catamaran, one hull was about 60 foot long the other was slightly shorter. Not out of planning you understand, but because of the length of the timbers they used for the keels. He told me the hulls were slightly, ever so slightly "toed in" this helped Ontong track sweetly and she could be set up to self-steer with ease.

She had a deck of thick untreated wide pale wood that stretched unbroken between the two hulls. This deck just begged to be trod on with bare feet. In fact, the whole boat was a symphony and celebration for wood and its charms. The hulls with their thick mahogany planks had been decorated by a master shipwright who wielded an adze with a skill long lost in more "civilized" countries, this maestro had cut a pattern of shallow egg sized indentations on the inside and the outside of all the hull's planks.

Down below the starboard hull was living accommodation - a large table to sit around eat and talk, a galley, racks for plastic containers of dried food stuffs, along with some bunks and storage in big blue plastic drums, for water. Paintings by Hans (and some by an ex "disturbed" girlfriend) some fresh yellow flowers in small glass vase, a hatchet near the ladder alongside a dead Avocet, nailed with great care to the bulkhead. The more I looked, the more I saw, and all of it I liked.

A 40 hp outboard was fixed to the stern. Battery charging was taken care of by a 50 watt solar panel. The other hull held a large music station with big speakers, some more bunks and cargo space. The rig was of great interest to me. The first time I had ever come across the "Crab Claw ". A short mast, (looking like a lighting struck tree in a desert), Supported a long top spar and an almost as long boom. The sail was home-made from old canvas. Han's claimed the sail was easy to make as it only had to be cut flat, the shape was controlled by the halliard tension.

We sat around the deck, talked and ate. We swapped jokes, laughed and drank red wine from thick Moroccan glasses - it was a fine evening. Hans said he would come over and have a look at what we were doing in the tent the next day, which he did.

He showed up about mid-morning had a look around and then dropped his bombshell "If you don't get out of here soon, this project will take over your life and you won't go sailing anymore. If I were you I would run now, while you can". I took his words seriously but there was no way I could go until the job was completed.

When he finally left for Morocco several months later we had become firm friends, I am sure our paths will cross again, and I look forward to that time.

My sanctuary from the mad world of boat-building

Chapter 42

Helen managed to find a month of free time and came over. Maybe it was the best month of my life so far. It did not start out so good, we had a huge row the first night. I slept on the saloon sofa, Helen in the cabin. In the morning the sun was shining, the sea blue and inviting, a mile away the village of Ferragudo's white painted church's bell rang out the hour. I asked Helen to stay and she agreed too. We became friends again. In fact, she became a very important part of the team - she would do the cooking, cleaning and fetching from the shops. I had two bikes then, so the first one I had bought I fixed up for her with a better seat and a rack with a basket on it. She had a big colourful sun hat that she would wear when she went off to the shops. Funnily the dogs left her alone, but they would always chase me.

One early Sunday morning, long before Helen liked to rise, I went on a kayak trip to the caves nearby. I went past Aqua vita, I saw Wulf who is also someone who cannot stay in bed on a sunny morning, and asked if he would like to see the caves. He said he would, as Steffi was in Germany and he was a bit bored. It was a perfect day for the caves - not much swell, and low water. Wulf was suitably impressed. We went to the beach after and I had a good swim. Then on the way back he asked if Helen and I would like to go for a sail to some other caves further along the coast. I paddled quickly back and collected her. We rode our bikes to the beach. Wulf answered my handheld radio call and came and collected us in his RIB. We had a truly wonderful time - Wulf knew the coast very well and took us close into the spectacular rocky sea scape, where we waved at the people trudging along the Cliffside paths and felt very wealthy! Wulf put Helen in charge of the yacht and we took the two on board kayaks into various caves, with Helen following with the Catamaran. After we had finished with the cave exploration and recovered the kayaks, I had a swim and then we sailed back. It was such a treat.

Later when Wulf dropped us back on the beach, I saw a man with a carbon jet powered surf board, I went and talked to him, and showed him pictures of what we were doing with carbon. He was very interested and even let me have a go on his board, which was wild because it was radically fast and easy to break. I did a quick lap of the anchorage, clinging on for dear life. I managed to return it back to where I had started from and thankfully gave it back in one piece to the owner. I was very impressed, and briefly toyed with the idea of buying one, asking how much they cost. He told me a new one cost £11,000! He also needed a modification done as he wanted foot straps fitted, and I told him we would do it if he brought it over. I was not surprised to see him a couple of days later when he came and found us in our lair. His name was Steffen, he was tall, good-looking man who had been in the German army as a parachutist but now worked for Siemens in Genoa. He was on holiday and spent his time surfing on his jet board or skydiving. Helen, Wido and I all liked him at once, so we agreed to help with his board. Helen had a quite word with me and told me not to screw up or it could get very expensive!

Opening up the board showed that it would not be possible to through bolt the straps, so we worked out a fix that involved bonding on two stainless steel 6mm bolts for each strap. Wido made two jigs out of waste glass fibre strips. I cut out the carbon strips we would use. I measured out the small amount of resin and hardener we would need then worked out the times. We would only have 12 minutes to complete the job once I had mixed the resin with the fast hardener because of the temperature. So we had to build the air tight bag first then open it up enough for us to both work. I had Steffan stand by with his watch so he could count down the minutes. After getting everything ready we started. It all went well and we finished with seconds to spare. Then after 30 minutes we put the vacuum on. A short time later it had all cured. We gave it a clean-up and Steffan took it home. I told him to leave it in the sun for a couple of days to harden off properly, but he used it the next day and was very pleased. I realised we were no longer carbon "beginners" but had become able to use the knowledge we had in different situations. Our work had blown Steffen away - he was running around telling his surfing buddies and calling us "carbon nerds"! He was also good enough to arrange for both Wido and me to meet him on the beach and have a go on his board. He even fitted the on-board Go-Pro camera and made a short film of us that he posted on You Tube! It was great fun.

Wido, Helen, myself and Steffan with the repaired carbon fibre jet board

Chapter 43

Weeks past, and slowly the work progressed. Richard ran into money problems, and struggled to pay me. Sometimes we ran dangerously short of materials. A pallet of goodies would arrive just in time. I was asked to give a talk at Liverpool Yacht club about the transatlantic trip on Gloria, so I took some time out and went. Very enjoyable it was too. Dave Harding, who organised it, asked me to talk for about an hour and a half. I had never talked so long before, but with Wido's help I went through my photos and loaded 100 of the best onto a flash drive, I only had to talk for a few minutes on each photo and the time would be spent.

The flight was easy, and Dave met me at the airport. His house was only a couple of miles away. We went out for dinner that night. In the morning I went running, in a nearby park. I explained to Dave that both my parents had come originally from Liverpool. They had lived near Sefton Park. So Dave lent me a mountain bike and we went for a ride. I had not realised it but I was only a mile or so away from the flat my parents had rented when they were first wed. We rode around the park and through the gardens created a few years ago when Liverpool was nominated as a Cultural centre, and very swish they were too. We then went onto the river front and the marina. We met a lot of people and saw a lot of boats - Dave was obviously as big a boataphial as I was! We had a great time and I was amazed at how clean and interesting Liverpool had become. The last time I had been there it was as fine an example of urban decay as you could see.

The talk went well. My Uncle Tony who I had not seen in many years showed up, along with my cousin Heather, who I had never actually met. She brought her daughter, a very pretty girl who yawned a bit while I was talking and showing my pictures. It all ran along smoothly and after about an hour and 10 minutes I was finished. Dave suggested that anyone with questions should ask them then. Another 20 minutes ran by as I answered some very good queries. The audience were still interested and no one had fallen asleep, even Heather's daughter said that she was determined to go sailing one day! I sold and signed books the rest of the evening then we went back to Dave's house and his charming wife Jeanette made us supper and I went to bed.

Returning to Basildon the next day by train was a relaxing affair, the country side looked very green compared to the landscape of Portugal. Helen and I had 1 whole day to ourselves before a very bad weather forecast persuaded me to go with Helen to Thurrock yacht club to see how things were going. I spoke to a few of my friends there including Dave (pigtail) who had taken over as Bosun from me, and as we were leaving I happened to say, "If you need any help, just ring". The nasty front came in during the early hours and two yachts broke adrift, my phone rang at 07.00 hrs, it was Dave taking me up on my offer. I put on some old clothes and borrowing Helen's car, drove down to the yacht club.

One yacht (Magic Star) was hard up against a sea wall where it had been blown at High Water which was about 06.00 that morning. Another one called Apollo had dragged its mooring which had become entangled with a small motorboat, both vessels were bashing against each other in the still very fresh breeze. I went into the Boson's office to change into something a bit warmer and found my old dinghy drysuit hanging where I had left it a year or so ago, so I quickly put it on. I went to drink a cup of tea with Dave while we were waiting for Dereck Lucas, the owner of Apollo to bring down his key. There was far less chance of us doing any damage if we used the yachts own engine to get her clear. Derek however was up the hospital, and by the time he made it down to us, his yacht's keel was almost touching the mud. Dave had his dinghy with its outboard ready, a big Polish guy who had recently joined the club helped us launch from the causeway. Waves were sweeping across the causeway, and there was no margin for error. We had to get off clean or be swept onto the drying mud banks ourselves. It was a good getaway, and we were soon aboard Apollo, with not a moment to lose, as the fast dropping tide was running in the same direction almost as the wind. Dave opened up the companionway and turned the electrics on, I turned the key and after quite a few revolutions the small motor caught. When I was satisfied it was running smoothly I asked Dave to cut the mooring ropes, which he did. I engaged forward gear and gave it full revs. The motor did not have enough power to push the bows through the wind and with the keel ploughing through the soft mud, she could not build up enough speed, but I won enough space for plan B, which was throw her in astern and used the tide and the wind to push the yacht past the motorboat and into deeper water. It worked and I even managed to turn her, and get us moving towards a vacant mooring buoy. We were soon secured to the mooring and went back ashore. The big Polish guy helped us get the dinghy back on its trolley, up the causeway and back to the club, getting a second drenching for his trouble.

I took Dave off for an early lunch up in the town of Grays, and we discussed getting the other yacht off the beach. This was a new situation for Dave. There were several barriers to a successful salvage. The yacht was in a place that a crane could not lift it, so it would have to be towed out to deeper water. However the tide that morning had been a neap (smaller tide), at 5.6 meters, and the next high water was even smaller at 5.5 meters. If you factor into that the wind which had been on the yachts beam pushing it sideways up the beach you can see the problem. The yacht would not have enough water to float. The forecast was of a couple of calmer days but then another blow at the weekend. It was either get her off the next tide or never.

There was a way of doing it and I outlined a plan to Dave. We would lay an anchor as far out as possible, with the rode to the bow and a spring to the stern - this would stop the yacht bashing against the sea wall if the rode and the spring were kept tight. Then the work boat would come in and take a line attached to a halyard, (attached to the top of the mast) then when I thought it was about slack water the work boat would haul us down almost onto the yacht's side, by going gently astern. The yacht would then no longer have its keel stuck in the mud and we should be able to motor off or be pulled off.

After lunch we went back down and started work. First job of all was to lay out the anchor. We commandeered a small pram dinghy and I put an anchor with some chain attached and a longish coil of rope. Donning my old dry-suit and double lashing my boots on, Dave helped me trolley the dinghy to where the yacht lay. We launched it off the wall and after making off the end of the coil I ran across the mud skimming the dinghy, speed was the key and keeping my weight off my feet. I reached the water and I dug the anchor in, before pushing the dinghy back up to the yacht. It was hot work, but I cooled down quickly in the cold wind with light rain thrown in. Russell Cherry and John Darby were helping the owner Jim to dig the biggest rocks out from around the keel and skeg. John helpfully mentioned that the last yacht that had ended up on that beach had been dragged over the sea wall by a crane and loaded onto a low loader to be sent off for land fill! I told Jim and the others of the plan, John wished us success but then had to go back to work. The rain started falling harder. Slowly as much of the rocks and mud were cleared as possible. The water had begun its return and we went back to the club for a cup of tea, a warm up and a meeting to brief everyone who would be helping. There were quite a few people.

Jim's family were there, but of limited use as they had not had much to do with boats, and a dirty night in the Thames is the wrong place to start. The treasury secretary Clare had showed up, and she was more useful, as was big Craig who is a paramedic as well as being big and strong. The Polish fella who had been so helpful before also showed. He, along with Dave (pigtail) and Clare made up the work boat crew, and Craig and Jim came with me back to the yacht. We climbed aboard and waited. It was cold and black before she started to move. Although she floated at about 18.00 her keel was still in the hole where we had removed the rocks and mud. Dave brought in Tango (the workboat) and we tried a tow, but it was no good. We waited some more, but at 18.15 the yachts on the moorings had swung to point their bows upstream, although the tide was not supposed to start ebbing until 18.45, I suspected the wind being Westerly would force it to cut early. So I called Dave up and asking him to approach from the downriver side of the anchor, to take our line attached to the halliard and pull us flat. Jim started up his engine. Dave had to have a few goes before he was in the right position, but when he was he did a great job of easing us gently over, and when we were at about 45 degrees I put the gear shift in ahead and we came off sweetly as you would like. Once clear we recovered the anchor and Tango let our line go. We were soon attached to a mooring and washing some of the mountains of mud off. Back in the clubhouse I had a celebratory cup of tea with the owner and his family and all those people who gave up their time for no reward and turned too on a cold wet night just to help, before driving back to Helen and a hot bath that I so badly needed.

Salvaging work at Thurrock Yacht club with 'Pigtail Dave'

Chapter 44

I managed a couple of days work on Gloria, (helped by Helen's grandson Charlie), now hauled out ashore at Brandy hole boat yard, and looking sad and unloved. I also managed a certain amount of dog walking with Boss, (Helen's son's staffie) before Helen and me were once more separated by my need to finish Trinity.

Back in Portugal we started on what I thought at the time was the last phase of the rebuild, taking the tacked on Port bow off, vacuuming on the final laminates, fitting the inside out with its furniture and finally vacuuming on three laminates of carbon fibre to secure it in place. It was hard work but hugely enjoyable. Every day we made progress. Once the bow was on, we started on the stern. Work that once was really challenging was now routine. We had begun to realise that the material was incredibly strong and the building we had done was of very high quality. Sometimes we had to trim back a bit of carbon to make parts fit, and it was always remarkable how strong it was. The strength came because of the mixture of components. The three laminates of carbon were two sheets that had their strands running at 45 degrees, and one sheet that's strands ran at 90 degrees. The core in the middle was very special stuff and once it was sandwiched between another three carbon laminates like the first and was held together with the very special Epoxy (Ampreg 21) we ended up with a light but stiff and strong shape, but only if the resin was mixed properly with the exact right amounts, and only if the temperature charts were adhered too. There were so many ways to mess up, but only one correct path, and Wido and I had trodden it for many months, despite the rains of winter and heats of summer. The end was now in sight and I looked forward to getting the time to work on Gloria and go sailing with Helen.

I returned to spend Christmas in Basildon with Helen. It was something of a shock, as the day before I was on my favourite beach catching some rays and cooling off in the wonderful blue ocean. The next day I was back in a very damp England, complete with crowded roads, jammed pavements and bad-tempered people. Christmas day was very good and my mother joined us as well. Helen cooked a splendid feast and everything ran smoothly. But after that perfect day things began to go wrong.

I went to see Trinity's owner Richard. We discussed the rebuild and he said he was very pleased with the work so far, but he also wanted the main hull rebuilt. I had been thinking the same thing myself, but it's one thing to toy with an idea, and it is another to face the reality, the extra time and added work. I knew Helen would be less than happy about me staying many more months. Originally I had told her I would be away for about three months, and it had already taken 14. I began to think it might well take another 12 months if we did have to remove the main hull in sections and using them as plugs, mould new parts as we had done with the outer hulls (Amas). Not only would the parts be much bigger, but the hull would have to be stripped of the mast, generators, battery banks, water maker, and all the electrical equipment.

Richard agreed to send Paul Wells out as a first step to a) ascertain if a total rebuild of the main hull was really needed, b) the most efficient way of doing such a thing, c) the quality of the work we had done so far and d) help us make a new shape for the stern of the main hull.

After the meeting I returned home and broke the news to Helen that I would be spending most of the next year in Portugal. I could see she was not very happy about that at all, but she agreed to return with me when I went back, and to stay a whole month. I booked plane tickets to return at the start of March for 5 days. I told her I would fix it so I was not away for longer than a month at a time and I thought that would be enough to see us through the coming year, but I could see she was less than happy and we had several rows over the next few days. Matters were not helped by the fact that I was madly busy, seeing my father, step mum, aunty Shelagh, Fred and everyone as well as going down the boat yard and trying to do some work on Gloria. The two weeks shot past and before I knew it we were back on a plane heading south. We had been unable to sit together on the plane, maybe which was a sign of what was to come.

We arrived back in Portugal on the 13th, and good old Wido was there to meet us at Faro airport. We stopped to drink coffee and also to buy oranges from a roadside vendor on the way back. Wido told me it had been raining since I left so we had not missed much work. We did some shopping at Lidl's and arriving back at Trinity. Helen got stuck into cleaning up the boat, on the second day I went into the main cabin and Helen put a small box of unopened condoms in front of me and asked "what's this" I tried to explain that I had bought them while I was in a pharmacy getting a water filter, even to me it sounded lame, but it actually was the truth, just a stupid impulse purchase. I pointed out the box was unopened, but to no avail. Helen became angrier and angrier, accusing me of all kinds of stuff. The problem was that I had started a particular difficult bit of carbon work with Wido, and the limits of our time until we had to apply the vacuum were fast approaching. If we did not get it on we would ruin a lot of work and have to spend days grinding the mess out. I did not have the time to attend to Helen, and on top of that poor Wido had to overhear everything that she was shouting. By the time the job was stabilised and I could send Wido home, Helen had packed her bags. Talking did not seem to do any good, and quite frankly I had had enough, I gave her all the euros in my wallet so she could stay in a hotel, and she left.

I expected her to calm down and call me up, but she didn't. She went back to the U.K. and it became very obvious that we were over. The future I had mapped out for us no longer existed, not just in that Helen would not be there with me but on my return from the Atlantic I had sold Gloria to Helen for £1, more of a gesture of solidarity than anything. With Helen gone, so was Gloria. As well as becoming homeless, I was boat less to boot. Helen continued her bad tempered war by giving all my possessions that were in her house to the charity shop. I did not want to leave Portugal and tried to come to some amicable arrangement. I though once she started to have to pay the storage fees for Gloria, she would give the boat back to me. I received something of a shock when I found out that she had actually found someone who wanted to buy Gloria and sold her. Despite all this I could not bring myself to hate the woman, I could see it from her point of view, and I realised she must have felt like she was being strung along. Funnily enough once I was over the initial hurt the loss of the material stuff was not as painful as I thought it would be. I was sorrier about hurting her than the hurt she caused me.

Chapter 45

I did not have time to mope about. The weather was dry and Paul was coming over the next week, so it was a rush to get as much done before the winter rains started up again. In the evenings after work I started taking my mountain bike out for rides to get some space and fresh air into my lungs. A couple of times I visited my beach and had an evening swim. The sea was colder and the waves more boisterous and never failing in their ability to wash away my troubles and make me glad to be alive.

Paul showed up and made himself at home, and he was pleased with the progress. The first day was spent with him tapping all the work we had done and marking any different sounding parts with a felt tipped pen. Once he had finished he asked me to get a grinder and get kitted up. He then chose 4 randomly marked parts and asked me to grind off the carbon until I hit the core. This I did, he then with a modelling knife attempted to separate the fibres. It was impossible, all the sites chosen showed good saturation of epoxy resin and the core had been penetrated with epoxy filler. We had passed that part of the test. The next part was to see if all the work we had done was straight, there would be nothing worse than to find out Trinity was lop sided on one Ama was higher than the other. The levels checked fine as well, much to our collective relief. Paul was really pleased - he had taken a big chance letting Wido and I loose unsupervised on such a complicated job, but it had all worked out.

Next we moved onto the main hull. We drilled core samples in all the sections, and the result was that the original build was well done, completely different from how the Ama's had been built, so apart from the bow section above the waterline and the stern, we could leave it alone. This was a huge relief.

We had a drawing from the Marine Architect Doug Hinge who Richard had paid to come up with a shape that we could build on the stern to solve several problems. These were namely a) to change the underwater shape at the very stern, the old one was a "V" shape and had little reserve buoyance, so as a result it did not resist being immersed and contributed to the vessel "pitching", b) because there was not a smooth transition from a round shape the old stern was causing turbulence and at high speeds a three foot "rooster tail" would follow Trinity around, slowing her up by the vast drag induced by the shape. Finally, c) Trinity had no easy access from the water onto the vessel, a good stern would be able to incorporate a folding ladder and make getting on-board far safer.

Under Paul's supervision we rigged battens and bent them around the old stern until we had a shape that was within the spirit of what had been drawn by Doug, if not to the exact dimensions. One of our problems was deciding exactly where the new waterline would end up. We had taken a lot of weight off by replacing 70% of the Ama's old build with carbon fibre/epoxy sandwich, but we did not know how much. I guessed that it would place Trinity back on the original waterline and found an old photograph that showed this. That was what we worked with. Once the area was marked out we rode our bikes to the building products store and bought a big pile of polystyrene blocks and melamine-faced hardboard. I arranged for this to be delivered and it arrived the next day. We could then start constructing the plug on which we could mould the new stern. I wanted to leave the old stern untouched because this gave an added safety factor, so should there be collision damage to that area in the future the main hull would still not be breached. For the minimal weight penalty of leaving a small part of the old build in place a whole new water tight bulkhead was designed in. We also decided to leave the polystyrene in place to act as a "crush" box after we had vacuumed on the carbon and core.

Apart from a couple of rainy days the worked proceeded well, and within a week the basic shape was in place but Paul had to again return to the U.K. I was very sad to see him go - he is a very easy person to work with and gets a lot done in a very short space of time.

Paul Wells, the carbon fibre expert working his magic on the carbon tubes for Trinity's steering gear

Chapter 46

I made a new friend on Facebook. Her name was Tricia, she expressed interest in what we were doing and I paid for her plane fare to come out. We really needed some help and to be honest I was very lonely. Things did not work out too good though. Tricia had hurt her back a couple of weeks before and was having difficulty getting up and down the ladder, as well as finding that the dust was setting off her asthma. Not only that, but I found the sight of her shampoos, soaps and other girly stuff in the forward heads strangely upsetting. After only two days I took her back to the airport and sent her home. I felt horribly cad-like. She was upset too, but I realised that my emotional problems would have to take a back seat while we got on with the job - I could not afford any distractions.

We still desperately need someone to help with the cooking and cleaning and shopping. Wido and I had worked best when Helen had been doing that. I was constantly stopping what I was doing to sort the lunch out or go and buy something, so I was pleased when a Portuguese lady who I already knew asked me if we needed any help. She also needed somewhere to stay, so I gave her the forward part of Trinity and a small amount of money each week for 4 hours work per day. This arrangement did not even cost Richard anything more on the payroll, because it meant I could stop working on Saturdays when I used to try and catch up with the cleaning. Paula was a really good cook and lunch became the high point of the day. In fact I had to ask her to ease up a bit as me and Wido were having difficulty staying awake after her big meals!

To solve the problem of being without a home or a boat I contacted my old sailing partner Peter Stower. We had jointly owned a

Trapper 500 called "Sarah" until I had borrowed £5000 off him to go sailing. I had never been in a position to repay him and had assumed he would sell Sarah to recoup his money that way. He told me he was going to be giving up sailing anyway and happily sold me the complete yacht for £6000. Richard promptly transferred this money into his bank account and I was a yacht owner again. Although Sarah was a lot smaller than Gloria at 27 foot, and as it looked like only myself would be going off sailing again, I now did not own anything other than a couple of holdalls of clothes and a few books, so she was big enough.

I hated being alone though, and one night while I was looking at Face book I saw a photo of an old friend, Eva. I was talking to her on F.B. and she told me she was also now single after her 25-year marriage had broken up. It seemed sensible to ask her out for dinner the next time I was in the country. So I did, and it was magic. We went to a Thai place near her flat in East Grinstead, we got in there early, and the next thing I knew it was 23.30 and the staff were packing up. The evening just flew past; we were both besotted.

I spent the Sunday working on Sarah and making lists of the work that needed to be done, but also thinking about Eva, I realised that I had found the woman that I would like to spend the rest of my life with, so on Monday I went back to East Grinstead and spent some more time with her. I still caught my flight on Tuesday, but I really did not want to go.

Sarah at Thurrock Yacht Club, with the old silly spade rudder

Chapter 47

I had been telling all my friends about how good Portimao was as a place to refit yachts in. I was clearly so convincing that in March, Martin Knightly and Ken Browning showed up in the boat yard, to check the place out with a view to bringing their own yachts down for some work.

Over a very good dinner cooked by our wonderful Portuguese cook Paula, the vaguest of plans was hatched. On the 6th of June 2014 both Ken and Martin would be at Plymouth waiting for a weather window to cross Biscay and then sail onto Portugal. As I also wanted to get my Trapper 500 Sarah down for some work I agreed to meet them there… It sounded easy at the time.

The next morning, I started the preparations. Crew was the most pressing problem. Sarah being a small yacht could only really take 2 or 3 people without getting very crowded, so there was no room for anyone who could not pull their weight. My first call was to Dave Norman, who had sailed with me on a couple of delivery jobs and been on the Trinity to Portugal job. He did a 12 years' stint in the British army and came out a sergeant. He is both physically large at well over 6 foot and never seems to stop smiling and cracking jokes no matter how bleak things get, and although he is not the most experienced of crew he is worth his weight in gold on any sailing trip. I was delighted when he agreed to come.

That problem sorted, I then started the planning so I could turn over all my work to my second in command Wido, for 1 month. That was the amount of time I reckoned I would need to recommission Sarah and get her launched and seaworthy. Then I had to run the plan by Richard the Trimaran's owner and make sure he was cool with it all.

Time hurtled past as it does and on the 24th of May I caught a flight back to Gatwick. My girlfriend Eva met me and we had a lovely precious few days together, during which I bought her a ring and we became engaged. Then I hired a van and drove over to start work on Sarah. She was still hauled out at Thurrock Yacht Club. I will draw a veil over the next few days, but the winter's work got done and we were only a day behind schedule and ready to splash on Saturday. The problem was that the tides had started to cut. I needed to get Sarah on a trolley down as far as possible and let the tide come in and float her off. Of course my old mate sod picked his moment to strike. The winch broke down and we could not lower the trolley down until it was fixed half an hour later. By which time the brown mud laden water had covered the slip and I could not get the trolley in the place I wanted. On top of that the tide (always a fickle companion in that part of the Thames estuary) was half a meter below prediction. So at 15.15 with no chance of floating off I took the rash decision to cast off the ropes to the trolley. Sarah fell out, I passed a spinnaker halyard via Chris Ashton to my mate who was standing by with the work boat, pigtail Dave put a steady pressure on the rope and pulled Sarah over so I could motor off. The trick worked just as well as when we used it to salvage "Magic Star" and I was able to motor off into deep water, and get underway.

Waving good bye, I caught the tide down the estuary to the Medway, and then caught the flood up to Hoo. I picked up a mooring and got some shut eye before Dave rang me at 03.00 and informed me that the water was up enough to make the entrance of the marina. I came in and parked up while we got his stuff on board and refuelled from a 20 litre can of diesel he had lying about. And so it was on the 1st of June we made our exit just as the sun was beginning to brighten the Eastern sky. It was nice to see the withies I had missed on the way in - funny how bits of scrappy stick can at times be so encouraging. Bacon sarnies followed before I passed the helm over to Dave and snatched another couple of hour's kip.

Into the Estuary with a light South Westerly giving us enough to sail all through the Princess channel and catch the tide to take us all the way to Dover before it slowly died. There being no future in attempting to do battle with a foul tide with no wind I elected to pull into the Anchorage at Dover for a few hours. After getting permission we proceeded though the Western entrance to the Anchorage, there in a moment of madness I committed the apparently mortal sin of mooring up to one of the orange buoys that everywhere else are used as mooring buoys, in Dover they are used to delineate where the big ship anchorage stops. I then proceeded to blot my copy book further by turning off my radio. Fairly soon after these hideous crimes had been committed a fishing boat was alongside, the occupants informed us that Dover port control would like to talk to us. I turned on my radio and received a no doubt well-deserved dressing down. Well, I expect they get a lot of practice doing that seeing as how none of the buoys are marked in anyway. We went off and anchored correctly, had a meal and got some sleep.

Later with the tide beginning to run in our favour we motored out, and chugged most of the night westwards. The on-going fishing challenge began once more. Last trip Dave in a total fluke pulled up 3 very large mackerel off the Spanish coast, and has been gloating about it ever since. But neither of us caught anything until later the next morning when we responded to an "any vessels in the vicinity of Newhaven" call from the coastguard. As we were within a mile I answered. We were directed to look for possible people in the water. Dave (an army trained spotter) grabbed his army binoculars and started calling out possible targets at various o'clocks. The "people" turned out to be "happy retirement" balloons. I was able to report that all survivors had been harpooned and were now on board before we were released with thanks to continue or voyage. We pulled into Brighton for some more go go juice before cracking on. The wind was still light but was forecast to blow from the S.W. later so I wanted to cover as much ground as possible in case we got stopped.

We made it through the Loo channel after a long day of tacking down the coast, and were there in time to catch the fair tide that helped us onward. Once through we could crack the sheets off and sail straight for our new destination, Gosport. We arrived at Hasler marina at 20.00 and went for a much needed meal.

It was blowing the next day, so we did jobs about the boat such as marking the anchor rope and measuring all the headsails I had on board and folding them up. We also changed the big Genoa for a flat cut working jib as I guessed there would still be some windward work ahead to be done. After that I tackled the A.I.S. problem. I had fitted one but it did not work. It did not take long to find out why - I had not linked the NASSA display to a GPS. My GPS did not have a feed wire (as it is very old) so I sought advice. At the local chandlery they offered me a new GPS for about £370! A nice man from Ocean Electrics advised me to try the chandlery at Port Solent. By then I had had enough, so we went to visit HMS Victory. It was brilliant and well worth the trouble.

The next day we went off to Port Solent marina and after locking in wandered up to the shop. They did have a cable, the very last in stock that would allow my emergency handheld GPS to send a signal to the A.I.S. Back on board we discovered that the wires were different colours than I needed. Garmin who I rang next were not very helpful, so the long suffering Mike of Ocean Electrics had to have a stab at talking me down from the desperate place I go when faced with anything electrical and expensive. It all turned out nice and as a bonus the Red arrows were doing a display nearby and we watch them for a bit before getting cleaned up, going for a good meal and afterwards watching the latest Tom Cruise movie. It was another great day and set us up nicely for the next leg.

It was still blowing briskly when we left with the last of the flood in the afternoon at 16.00hrs, but the forecast was for the S.W. to gradually fade away before a S.E. wind started to pick up the next morning. We had a terrific sail down the Solent - the flat cut jib was a joy to use on short tacks, and Sarah was easy and light on the helm. But by Hurst we had to change back to the big Genoa as the wind was fading with the daylight. We motored through the rest of the night. Off Portland Bill we were in time to catch the fair tide, and with the day light also came the breeze from the S.E. We tore across Lime bay on a broad reach just under the Genoa as the main was not needed. By the time we flashed past Start Point the sea was getting up and the wind was about force 6 and still building. I pulled in close the Bolt Tail to lose a bit of the sea and in flat water Sarah hit an honest 7.8 knots for a while leaving a huge wake and stunning me with her cheekiness, after all she only has a waterline length of 22 foot or so...

It did not take us long to get into Plymouth. Martin was already there with Bonny, his Fisher 34, and Ken arrived just after us with

Splendid, his moody 34 centre cockpit. I missed his arrival as I was diving under Sarah, clearing her prop of a branch that had fouled it. We had made the 6th of June target, and no one was more surprised than me!

I was born in Plymouth and have family still living there. My Mother and my sister Anna who came down to visit did not get a lot of sense out of me because I was very tired, but I did agree to have dinner with my mother at her flat the next evening. Dave and I slept the deep sleep that night. The next day was frantic - it was still very fresh outside so we had a day to both sort things out and see relatives and friends. My brother Toby showed up, and insisted in making us proper coffee with his portable hand operated pneumatic coffee machine, complete with tiny unbreakable cups. After he left another brother Matt rowed over with a sick outboard. He fixed it while we talked and then accompanied us to "Bogey Knights" the army surplus store of legend that is a mere mile or so from Mayflower marina. We did not buy anything there because the proprietor seemed to have lost the ability to haggle, except for a couple of hardwood broom handles. Using these Matt and I engaged in a stick fight in a wonderful bit of parkland overlooking the Hamoaze. By then Dave was given to observe that insanity did not just run in my family, it seemed to amble taking it's time to get to know each member individually ....

Richard Ayres paid us a visit. He is an old mate from years ago, and also the owner of Kochi, a newly built solid teak bronze fastened pilot cutter - the man has taste! It was good catching up with him. Then when he went Dave and I dashed off to do some shopping. First stop was the fishing tackle place for secret weapons! Then, onto the supermarket for food. After that we made it to my Mum's for dinner and to meet my Niece Sarah, and her beautiful daughter

Noah, before dashing back for another dinner and drinks on board Splendid with the other crews. It was a funny night - I remember laughing a lot, not exactly about what but I do remember it was funny.

The next day brought a slight headache and a dilemma. The forecast was for light S.E. winds that would increase and go S.W. later and get up to force 6 with added torrential rain. But in the South of Biscay the wind was a charming N.E. and sunny. The other two skippers elected to go to L'abewrach in Brittany. But that did not suit Sarah or me as it would be an engine job with lots of slamming. Instead I said we would sail out until we could get a slant that would let us clear Ushant and its busy shipping lanes.

We left after once more putting the flat cut jib back on the forestay, and we were glad that we did. That night was not very pleasant, but much better than the next one. However, two things made life bearable, one was that the forecast was spot on and 75 miles west of Ushant the wind went S.W. and we could shape a course for Lorient, the other was that Sarah, good Sarah with the flat cut jib and the main rolled down to the first batten was gambolling over the big waves like a young and happy dolphin! She was a joy to steer. By the afternoon of the 10th June we were well inside the bay and clear of all problems when the wind started to fade. After changing to the Genoa we kept the speed up for another few hours before we became becalmed. I rolled away the foresail and started the engine.

It ran for 20 minutes before spluttering to a stop. I soon found the problem - water in the diesel. In fact, there were gallons of water in the tank and filters. We traced the problem to a badly sited breather. In the bad weather it must have been underwater half the time. By the end of the tank and filter cleaning session we had 15 litres of clean diesel left and an engine that was still reluctant to start. We first flattened the house 12 volt battery before moving on to the cranking battery. Dave drew my attention to a contact that had appeared on the A.I.S. screen set for a 4-mile range. I read the name and called up FV FLECHA and got no response. We started another round of bleeding, still no joy, but clean diesel was now coming out the cracked injectors. I called the F.V. again, still no response although it was very visible by then. Another few cranks and she fired on one before stopping, I told Dave to rest the battery, then one more go and she thankfully caught before settling down to a smooth fast tick over. I let her warm up before I put the gear shift over and we moved out the way as Fletcha thundered past - a couple of hundred tons of steel moving at 12 knots with no-one to be seen on watch. We had a cup of tea before setting the course on the tiller pilot and starting the clean-up.

Ten hours later I turned off the motor and set sails that would make the best use of the light N.E. zephyr that had got up. Our speed gradually increased but our course was 240 degrees when really we wanted 210, so I rigged a light weight flying jib poled out to windward and rolled away the main. Better than a spinnaker when two tired men are all the crew, Sarah firmed up and headed for Corunna. 240 miles rolled past and encouraged by hordes of happy dolphins and the wonderful blue sky /sea and warm sunshine we settled into an exuberant state of mind.

On the morning of the 13th of June the fog shifted to reveal Corunna in all its glory. After getting tied up in the marina we went for a well-earned meal ashore and to pay respects to the Tower of Hercules, the oldest lighthouse in the world and my favourite building ever. By the time we arrived back on Sarah we just managed to have a bite before falling asleep in the early evening. All thoughts of a run ashore faded in favour of a soft duvet.

Bonny and Splendid came in 16 hours after we did, so we went to the other marina to meet them. That night we had a hilarious get-together that involved a wee bit too much fall over juice and resulted in the launching of the W.A.F.I. (Wind Assisted Flipping Idiots) sailing club - apparently I am the Commodore. ….

My head did not ache too much the next morning, and we had somehow acquired a large box with a tasty looking pizza in it for later which was good. I stumbled up to have a shower and look at the forecast. The brit with the Halberg Rassy opposite us thought he would stay for the next week or so on account of the wind, but when I looked at the forecast pinned to the gate it looked fresh but the wind was N.E. going East. So I saw no reason to linger. After a shower I paid the dues and went to find Dave and tell him the glad news.

We set off and once clear of the pier heads set just the genoa. Sarah sailed along at about 4.5 knots steered by the tiller pilot. Dave and I had plenty of time to take pictures and admire the scenery. Gradually the N.E. wind got up and I reefed the genoa. But we still had far too much sail up, and by the time we arrived of Finisterre we had already had one well-deserved knockdown and washed out the cockpit... The sea had become quite large and when a catamaran overtook us with a very deeply reefed main Dave managed to get some impressive photos. I had the helm all day, as we were surfing at up to 12.4 knots at times. I felt that the privilege of getting it all wrong should belong to me, buy thankfully by the time we rounded the cape and put the wind on our beam none of the really nasty seas had caught us badly.

I was super knackered when I handed the helm over to Dave. I had foolishly taken some of the rolls out of the genoa thinking the wind had begun dropped down in a temporary lull. When I crawled back into the cockpit at about midnight Sarah was once again very hard pressed and Dave was struggling to stay on course. A few more rolls sorted this out and Sarah regained her manners. The wind gradually died off after dawn. We arrived in Bayonna at 06.00 having covered the 115 miles in 20 hours. Sarah had once more impressed both Dave and me with her speed and sea kindliness. We anchored, stripped and went swimming, and then after a quick bite went to sleep.

I think it was the silence that woke me - that or the warm sun that was slanting into my face. It was 12.30 and time to go. We felt refreshed by our sleep and ready for anything. There was not a breath of wind so we motored along at 3 knots trying unsuccessfully to catch fish. It was the 17th of June and we faced light winds for the next couple of days as we meandered down the Portuguese coast, sometimes for a few hours we could sail but mostly we had to use the engine. Although we had filled up in Corunna the tank is only small, taking about 25 litres, and the diesel can only held 15. I became a bit concerned on the morning of the 19th when we were only about 30 miles from Cape St Vincent. I reckoned that we needed 14 hours of fuel if we motored all of the next 60 miles at 4 knots or so. Dave had the brilliant idea of adding our stock of cooking oil to the diesel to give us another 4 litres of juice. At that time there was not a breath of wind and the sea totally flat. Needless to say as soon as we had carried out this cunning wheeze and I was looking for something to fry the breakfast with, the wind came back!

We could just lay St Vincent, our friends the dolphins came back for more games and all was well. After rounding St Vincent our course became a dead run so I gave the spinnaker an airing, Dave had never sailed under a kite before and was really taken with the experience. Well, he would have had to have been dead not to have, as we were zipping past the beautiful Algarve coast at 6 knots through the bluest sea while the sun shone on. It really does not get much better than that. We even made it to the marina at Portimao in time to get a meal in one of the restaurants that was still open. The food tasted superb as well deserved grub does. It was the crowning glory of a beautiful sail.

Sailing Sarah to Portugal, with Dave Norman

Chapter 48

I was now able to take Wido out sailing at the Saturdays, he had sailed dinghies as a boy, but never in a yacht. He is a natural helmsman so was easy to teach. On Sundays I took my good friends Chris and Ana sailing. The only fly in the ointment was that I kept Sarah alongside a wharram cat owned by a strange German man. This was on the part of the dock that fishing boats and yachts moored while they waited for repairs or a space to lift out into. Senor Rossa said it was okay for us to be there but the German apparently did not like his view being obstructed. He started out by telling me that I would have to pay 25 euros a day to stay there. Then he wanted me to leave a gap of 1.5 metres between our boats. This continued for four weeks.

Paul came back for another visit and I lent him Sarah so that he and Martin Knightley could go for a sail. While they were away I was embroiled in a row with someone in the yard. Unfortunately, I did not handle the situation very well and it turned into a loud argument. I was getting over that when I went over to take the ropes and help Paul and Martin moor up to the German. He started griping and shouting at me because there was a fishing boat badly fendered bashing his boat - somehow this was supposed to be my fault. The red mist descended and I said some unfortunate things, and in the middle of all this Sarah arrived. Paul was not pleased to see me falling out with people in the area.

I had Sarah lifted out a couple of days later and started work on her. I built her a new rudder and designed and had fabricated a stainless steel trim tab wind activated steering gear. The stainless steel work was done by a very clever English man also called Paul. I worked on Sarah in the evenings and weekends, but this had a big disadvantage. We had always tried to only work with the epoxy every other day. But now I was getting a double dose my body started to react with it. One Saturday my whole face swelled up like a football. About this time I realised I had lost my sense of humour. Trying to regain it involved re-launching Sarah with her new rudder. Eva managed to get some time off and came down for a week. She had her first sail ever, and was very impressed. We anchored in the bay near Ferrigudo and left the hatch open while we talked and watched the stars. To be afloat again with the woman I loved on a boat that was now rigged to sail long distances was a glimpse of the life I really wanted.

The sea trials were a complete success. Sarah was transformed by the new rudder, and the self-steering worked and promised even better performance in the future. Alas, Eva had to return home, and I went back to work but kept Sarah in the marina at Portimao, using her as my new base and leaving Paul the huge aft cabin on Trinity for his accommodation. Sadly, things did not work out. I could not settle down, and Paul took me to one side and told me he was not very happy with some of the work I had done in the last few months and that he really felt it was time for me to go. I was not alone. Our cook Paula was also surplus to requirement and a small black kitten I had name "Carbon" received her marching orders too. It was no trouble to re-home the cat, a nice family from Lisbon claimed her. Paula moved onto another yacht.

Once I got over the shock I realised that Paul was right. I had become bad tempered and snappy and I was disrupting the morale of the work place. I consoled myself with the thought that I had done what the owner had originally asked to do, i.e. find the personnel who could do the job and put them in place. Both Wido and Paul were people I had found. At the end of the day boat building was not what I really wanted to do, and forcing myself to stay there and do it was having a detrimental effect on me. This was all compounded by now having a vessel I owned that could to go places on my doorstep.

I went back to the U.K. again to see Eva. It was October and if I rushed I could be ready for a sail to some far off place. Pete Evans an old pal sent me an e mail to say he had a set of self-tailing winches that would fit Sarah in Carriacou, so the Caribbean seemed like a reasonable destination. Eva was too busy to be able to come with me but she selflessly urged me to go and have a good time.

The week after I arrived back on Sarah was very hectic, as I filled her with food water and two full Gas cylinders. I also had to sell the stuff I would not be able to take with, me such as my mountain bike and my kayak. I was feeling very fit and after agreeing to sell the bike to Paul the welder I took it for one last blast. On a steep downhill tight right-hand bend on a gravel road I discovered that my ability to fly is still not as good as I could wish it to be. I hit the ground very hard and for a little while could not move. When I came round I realised that the bike was not as hurt as I was. Blood was seeping out of various grazes on my face and head and hands and from the pain when I breathed I knew I had damaged a rib or two. Not really what I wanted to happen a few days before a big sail. I slowly rode the bike back to the marina and then went and had a shower to wash the blood and dirt off, ignoring the stares that I was receiving from various people on the way.

I had by that time bought a satellite tracking device so I could let Eva know where I was. My plan was to leave on the Sunday and sail the 750 nautical miles to the Canary island of Gomera. The weather forecast was for light winds on Sunday but getting stronger on

Monday, and then blowing 30 knots or so on Tuesday. I wanted to test Sarah in strong-ish winds just in case there were any unknown problems. Strong winds early in the sail suited this plan and I felt my injuries would not hamper my ability to sail Sarah. So I continued getting her ready. On the Friday I left the marina and anchored in the bay.

On Saturday night I had a final dinner with my good friends Chris and Ana in their lovely house that almost overlooks the bay in the beautiful village of Ferrigudo. They were worried for me - they could see I was a bit second-hand and Chris had seen the weather forecast. He thought I should stay a bit longer. But my mind was made up and I left the next morning, slowly sailing past my good friends Wulf and Steffi in there Catamaran "Aqua vita" and Louie and Karen in "Rita" and then past the breakwater where Chris and Ana stood waving and taking photos.

I always feel horrible when I leave on a big trip. I hate to say "goodbye" and this was even worse; not only was I leaving behind good friends, the very best of friends even, not to mention a beautiful woman who loved me England, but I had become very attached to that part of the Algarve, its beaches and its people. For a while I seriously contemplated turning around, but like many a mariner before me found, it's the far horizon that exerts a pull that is stronger (just) than the comfort of the life left behind. I set the course and trimmed the sails and we were bound for Gomera. Our track was a bit zig zaggy as I still had not mastered the self-steering gear but at least it would make us harder for a torpedo to hit!

I caught a fish the first night and ate it for dinner and breakfast. Then the weather started and with it came waves of pain, my damaged ribs would not let me rest and my head ached constantly.

But once I stowed the mainsail and reefed the genoa, Sarah steered herself towards our destination. After a few days the wind dropped down to something a bit more civilised and gradually the waves eased down to lumpy rather than monstrous. At 18.00 hrs each evening I pressed the buttons on the sat tracker and sent my current position. Both the rudder and the self-steering had no problems. I became used to setting up the self-steering so the zig zaggy course became less of a ragged 40 degrees either side of our desired course to something a bit more like 15 degrees, which is almost acceptable in a new helmsman and not uncommon in a mechanical steering device even if its cost thousands, so I was quite pleased.

Tenerife hove into view after six days, as expected. What was not anticipated was a call for "sailing vessel Sarah" by Tenerife traffic control. I tried calling back but they could not receive me. Once I got a phone signal I was able to ring Eva. She broke the news that after the first two sat messages I had sent and time coincident with the bad weather, no-one had been getting my signals! Chris and Ana had contacted her and from Portugal and they had also contacted the coastguard, Eva and my brother had spoken to Falmouth coastguard and even though I was by no means overdue a full scale search involving Portugal, Spain, Morocco and of course the UK had swung into action!

I made Sans Sabastian marina in Gomera very early the next morning. I would have waited before coming into a strange marina in the pitch darkness with a strong North wind blowing but I felt that if someone was trying to find me my duty was to make contact A.S.A.P. and the Coastguard was not receiving my VHF transmissions. My entrance was a bit manic, there was not a lot of space and lots of expensive posh yachts and sports fishing boats berthed in most of the bigger slots, but I spotted an empty finger berth, caught sod napping, and was tied up securely and safely before he woke up. A security man showed up to shine a torch on me and ask me why I had not called beforehand on the VHF. In fact, I did see the sign with the VHF channel to call, but I was already in the marina by then and in any case there was something more pressing on my mind, but my Spanish and his English were both not up to me explaining that the coastguard was looking for me.

I had to wait for the morning. At 09.00 sharp I was in the marina office, my attempts at injecting a bit of urgency into the checking in proceedings were met with a Spanish "take it easy, it's Sunday you hyper English idiot "sort of approach. Once the paper work was done I asked if they could call the coastguard for me. Lots of shoulder shrugging went on but no number could be found, I was directed to an office near the ferry terminal. But it was shut because it was Sunday. I phoned Falmouth coastguard in the end and spoke to a man who was disturbingly familiar with the situation, in fact he said "I strongly suspected you didn't have a problem but with all the calls we got we decided to use this as an exercise between the various countries"! He went on to say that they had had a number of similar problems with this kind of tracking device. He promised to let everyone involved know I was safe and sound and in Sans Sabastian. After all this drama I had some breakfast and a nap. On emerging to go and look for my mate Mike Tattersfield who had Face book messaged me to say he also would be in Gomera on his way to Brazil. I was suddenly accosted by a small mob of the marina staff, who were very excited and told me that the coastguard was looking for me!

My old mate "Flying" Mike and his wonderfully restored Rival 32 Cymreiges where berthed not far from me, so I went over for tea -

it was good to see him again. He had arrived the day before. Mike cooked us up bangers and mash that evening after I went and found a friend of Eva's, whose other half owns a large posh yacht that has that marina as its base. Maureen and Noel were very friendly and pleasant people. They kindly invited both Mike and me to have dinner with them the next evening.

There are a lot of mountains in Gomera. We wanted to see a bit of the rest of the island and Mike decided a mountain bike excursion was in order. He is from Yorkshire and used to be very bicycle mad. He only gave them up to globe trot with the Royal Navy, and even then he kept buying them and shipping them back to home! So we went to a bike hire shop and were kitted out with a reasonable bike each, helmet, and spare inner tube for a ten euros. The guy ominously warned us that riding in Gomera was not like riding in Yorkshire. He also told us to stay away from the off-road tracks as the rain would make them very slippery.

Once outside of the town the road became a steep uphill gradient, and stayed like that for several hours' and 20 kilometres! My legs were on fire and cramping up and my ribs aching as I doggedly followed Mike upwards and ever upwards. Finally, we arrived at a "T" junction that showed another road back to Sans Sabastian. A look at my GPS showed we had climbed almost 1 mile above sea level! The descent was very scary, my glasses were not working very well in the rain, and the road was a mass of hair pin bends. The surface was as slippery as a young conger eel's tummy and the bikes tyres were very knobbly. To add to the fun, the drop in temperature to our legs from extreme effort to just resting in cold mountain rain caused the muscles to go into spasm - it effected Mike most and we had to stop while he felt compelled to lay down in the road and scream, causing the passing traffic to phone for help! After a while he recovered, and a lady who had driven from a nearby village to render assistance was assured Mike was once again fit for more bike riding and we were able to continue our rapid descent. As we got lower the light rain stopped (it was caused by us being in a cloud, we were so high up) the sun came out and dried the road nicely. Mike disappeared on ahead while I followed at a sedate pace more fitting for a man of my years and cowardice.

Sarah's new carbon fibre rudder. Steelwork by Paul of Onyx

Chapter 49

Having survived the mountain bike excursion, it was my turn to cook dinner. This was enjoyed in the cockpit while watching the sun go down, and our sore legs very grateful for the rest and tummies thankful for the food. We agreed to have the next day just for sorting out the boat and final shopping, and then to leave for the Cape Verde island of Sal the day after that. I asked Mike for a look at his charts as I did not have much information about Sal. He was amazed that I did not have all the charts of everywhere and rectified that discrepancy by downloading onto a flash drive all the charts of the world for me. Then by downloading a program called "open CPN" onto my laptop, I suddenly had all the data I needed to sail anyplace (as long as the laptop worked)!

Sarah and I had been dragged kicking and screaming into the modern world. But I was still glad to have all my paper charts stowed away just in case.

I spend the next day saying goodbye to the hospitable Maureen and Noel, shopping for last minute food stuffs and filling the water tanks. I also had a good look at the manual for the tracker and realised that I had been operating it incorrectly. The printed instructions on the side of the unit told me to press certain buttons until various lights lit up. In the manual it added that these lights were to be left to stay green until another little light ceased flashing, which in certain circumstance could be a while. "Doh!" I had not been leaving the thing on long enough - what had worked on trials in the marina while the boat was not moving, was not good enough while we were bobbing about at sea.

Departure day arrived with a weather forecast of mostly light winds and lots of sun. Once all was ready I motored over to the fuel berth when I saw it was empty. It only needed 10 litres to top up my tank, much to the operator's disgust who had to be summoned from his den in an office a short walk away. He went back to his cave while Mike was on his way to quench his vessel's appetite for go go juice. Once all was connected up and the surly fuel man again on station, Mike took 100 litres top up his tanks and fill a couple of cans that lived on the deck.

At last we could leave. For the first two hours the island's wind shadow precluded any sailing, but as soon as I saw the wind hawk on the mast start to point astern I cut the noise box and deployed the Genoa. Progress was very, very slow at first and difficult to get the self-steering set up, but gradually our speed picked up from 2 knots to 3 plus. Mike elected to keep steaming and soon disappeared over the horizon. Sarah covered only 50 miles for that day. Progress became steadier the next if a little rolly as the swells were back I had handed the mainsail the first few hours, so we were just under a poled out Genoa.

The next seven days were filled with down-wind sailing in classic trade wind conditions, accompanied with sun, warmth and the occasional Dorado that fell to my rod and line. They are my favourite fish to eat, their dramatic vibrate colours that fade to grey when they die never fails to sadden me, but the taste of them makes up for that (although probably not to the fish). I was able to speak via the VHF radio to yacht called Wildevaart one night, when they realised they were talking to the sailing yacht Sarah, they informed me that there was a search for us... I explained everything and looked forward to meeting up with them as they too were on their way to Sal. We also had a guest. A stormy petrel was found in the bucket I had left on the cockpit sole one morning. I took it out but the terrified creature hid away under a coil of rope trembling with fear. So I left it alone until the next day. When I picked it up carefully and holding it up so it could see sea, it opened its wings and gracefully flew off. I hoped it did not have a mate that was 100 miles behind us wondering where its buddy had gone.

The island showed up the day before we arrived, and I could see that it had a very tall peak. The wind dropped off to nothing, meaning a bit more motoring for the last of the miles. Rounding the break-water I saw Mike's bright yellow hull. It is a colour that stands out really well. There was space to anchor ahead of him, so I did so in five metres. I soon had the dinghy out and went to say "good morning" He was pleased to see me and we had breakfast together. He had arrived 36 hours before me but had used his engine (which is a Beta 3 cylinder 20hp lump that runs like a sewing machine) for 58 hours, whereas I had used "iron topsail" for only about 5. So I reckoned it was a draw.

Mike Tattersfield and myself at the top of a mountain

Chapter 50

We went ashore to the airport so I could check in. The contrasts from the last place we had been where very apparent. Gomera is part of Europe and Sal is part of Africa - a mixture of joy and optimism mixed in with squalor and poverty, kids that laughed and played diving off the top of an old fishing boat into the sea, old men watching the world go by from shaded spots, through eyes that reflected apathy and despair. Vibrant colours on painted buildings, with lurid reds and yellows, next to the grey of unadorned breeze blocked walls and rusty corrugated iron roofs.

We found a mini bus to take us to the airport. The fee was 3 euros, and although the currency is escudos nobody turned away euros, however the change was always in the local currency. The coins all have sailing vessels on them and are very pretty. The paperwork was processed by a friendly man and I had my passport stamped with an entry stamp.

We elected to walk back and see a few of the sights, which was a little difficult as any mini bus that passed tried to get us as a fare. Fortunately, Mike speaks Portuguese and was able to explain our strange behaviour of walking. We stopped at a super market and did some shopping. I was appalled at how expensive everything was. A tin of peas was twice as expensive as in Portugal and I thought the shops there were pricy! We then caught a taxi to the harbour and rowed back out to our boats. After a short rest we went ashore so that Mike could show me where the internet café was and I could catch up with my e mails and talk to Eva. To my relief I found that my tracker had been working just fine and Eva knew exactly where I was. Once we had finished there we went for a beer and omelette with fries before I headed back to Sarah to get some kip.

The next day the yacht I had spoken to on route (Wildevaart) came in. Mike already knew the crew from another port in the Canaries. There were 4 of them, all Dutch, and that night we had a sort of riotous party that culminated in all of us partaking in the local grog, (Mike of course knew where to go to get it!). I say it culminated there, but it's more accurate to say that my memory of events culminated there. I had my camera with me, and there are a whole heap of photos in places I don't remember being in!

Daylight revealed that Wildvaarte's dinghy had gone AWOL. This was serious, as dinghies are difficult to replace in places like the Cape Verdes and very expensive if you have to buy a new one. The skipper and another crew swam ashore to see if they could find it. The positive point was that the wind had not been totally blowing to seaward that night, so it might be someplace in the big harbour.

They showed up some hours later rowing their dinghy back - some kids had found it drifting about in the early morning. Big relief all round!

I spent the day doing more internet things in the café and buying some provisions. I could not get bread because that was only available early in the morning. I took the shopping back to Sarah and then went to get water, which was only available at the community fountain and gated. It is run by two old ladies who charge a pittance for you to fill your container. Here was another contrast for someone like me from a wet land where the rains frequently fall - in these islands the rain might not fall but once or twice in a whole year! There has been a desalination plant built lately and made the islanders lives a little less bleak, they no longer die of thirst. But it is still regarded quite rightly as a valuable commodity.

I did not join the party that night as we were leaving the next day to go to Mindello on the island of St Vincent. It was 120 miles away, and the forecast was for brisk N.W. winds. I wanted to be up early to buy bread and eggs, and did not relish another thick head!

Mike had to go to the police station and get his ship's papers back and I had also go there to pay a fee, hand in my ships papers and get them back again! All this was performed with good humour and we were separated from another 8 euros or so each....

Then we set sail. I was at sea first and I waited for Mike to come out. We spent some hours taking photos of each other. There was a 3 metre swell running and the blue Ocean, crisp white foam and bright sunshine made for dramatic photos.

The two yachts, although similar in many ways, are very different. The rig is the same - a simple sloop. But Sarah is slightly smaller and about half the weight of Mike's Rival. Most of the time I find it easiest to sail Sarah down-wind with just the genoa set. Mike had his genoa and full main out, and he was slightly faster. I deployed a heavily reefed main and we started to creep past him. Bearing in mind the forecast, and after I had satisfied myself that we could beat Mike If I wanted to, I struck the main and made things snug for the oncoming night so I did not have to worry about the steering. Mike and his yacht slowly forged ahead. Over the darkness the wind came on and we were under only a small handkerchief sized jib when dawn revealed the large amount of flying fish that had crash landed into the cockpit during the night.

The dramatic islands were in sight with first light, and during the course of the morning we swept past the very obviously volcanic produced outcrops of terra firma in a wild and boisterous sea.

Rounding the headland into the bay we gained the sanctuary of smooth water, but a terrific gust hit us and destroyed the light plywood wind vane I had made in Portimao. That was our only damage, and soon I was approaching the anchorage. I saw Mike, he had already been in for an hour and a half and had definitely won that leg which with the boisterous conditions favoured the heavier yacht.

The best place for me to anchor was some way astern of him. I turned Sarah about accordingly and put the wind (that had dropped down) behind us, then I took the engine out of gear and walked forward to sort the anchor out. I had just opened the anchor locker when another terrific gust hit us, and Sarah turned hard to port and accelerated up to about 6 knots, with an obvious intention to T bone an innocent French yacht. I legged it back to the helm, thinking I was far too late, throwing the tiller hard over to turn us to starboard and ramming the gear shift into hard astern at the same time. The French skipper appeared and was also able to fend off and we only touched with the lightest of glances, and while I stood off the skipper verified that there was no damage.

I anchored astern of him and went over with a bottle of wine to apologise for giving him such a shock. We shook hands and parted friends. Luckily Mike had not seen this otherwise I would have been in for some severe leg pulling.

Mike makes a friend in the Cape Verdes

Chapter 51

Mindello had hardly changed in most ways since I was last there with Gloria three years before. My first venture ashore was to get a gas cylinder refill. I landed my dinghy on the beach and dragged it up beyond the high water mark. Almost at once a local was there to say he would keep an eye on it for me. The petrol station a few metres away stocked the cylinders and I was very pleased to find that they only cost €4.50 - a bit different than the £32 I was charged in the U.K.!! I did some other shopping and went back to the dinghy. The guy hassled €1 out of me for minding my dinghy, and I rowed off to get Mike as we both needed to check in and find an internet café.

Mike did not want to land his inflatable on the beach because of possible damage and he had found out there was a pontoon we could use that was run by a dive centre. We tied up there and went off to enter the port legally.

It all took a bit of time and our ships registrations were retained, but the lady who carried out the paper work was fun so it was not too irksome.

We went off and did the internet thing. The guy who had looked after my dinghy spotted us and tried to fasten himself to us and when we tried to get rid of him he demanded payment for his "guide" services. He was difficult to shake off and followed us to the internet café. When we left he was waiting for us and kept up with yammering for money. Until Mike shouted at him and he finally got the message that he was not getting any more money out of us. This kind of thing was how I remembered Mindello from last time. It's very ugly and I think unnecessary. There were a large number of yachts anchored in the bay, and everyone needed to go ashore for fresh produce, water, and stuff like that. None of the locals were rowing up and asking if we needed anything. That would have been a service worth paying for, so it is not like there is no way for people to earn an honest dollar.

One of the e mails I sent was to a man called Alberto who I had met in Portimao. He and his son had a beautiful Catana catamaran which they were preparing for a world cruise. I wanted to know where they were. As luck would have it, they sailed into Mindello the next day, and anchored right astern of me! It was good to see them, and over dinner that night we caught up. Afterward we sung along to Dire Straight songs played by Pedro Barroso a brilliant musician, who was flying back the next day. It was a wonderful night and so good to be surrounded by happy people - Alberto, Daniel his son, his wife their daughter and Pedro.

The forecast was not so good for an Atlantic crossing - the trade winds were a bit patchy and light, but they are only a forecast. I had a hunch I would find enough wind for Sarah to make progress, so I changed the Genoa for and old light weight one and started get ready to leave later on that afternoon. I had noticed a small Gaff rigged boat in the anchorage and went over to see if it was being sailed by a friend of Paul Wells. It was, and we had a good natter and swapped books. His name was Rob and he knew Battlesbridge well, and we had several friends in common. He also was going to hang on because the light winds would not favour his ferro-cement gaffer that was only 24-foot-long yet almost twice Sarah's weight.

Mike was also going to wait a bit. He was bound for Brazil and his trip was only 1500 miles, so he had stacks of time before Christmas. Sarah and I departed at 14.00. The wind was bang on the nose at first until we cleared the harbour, then gradually it came round until it was on the starboard quarter. There was not enough to fill the heavier canvas of the mainsail, but the lightweight genoa set and pulled us along. A few times I had to start the engine to keep us moving but I was pleasantly surprised to find our first 24-hour mileage to be 92.

Once we were clear of the land masses our speed increased and the next day we covered 108 miles. Sarah was being a total babe. Putting the lightweight genoa up was what she needed, and as it was on the rolling furling reefing was a doddle - just a matter of easing the sheet and hauling on the reefing line. As the wind came more aft I started using the spinnaker pole to keep it from flapping when she rolled and she became even more stable. If I used a second genoa set flying and poled out with the main boom she would go faster but became less stable and yawed about more. It was far easier to lose a knot or so but have a gentle stress-free sail than crack on and possibly break something.

I settled into the lifestyle over the next week. The fresh fruit was eaten as it became over ripe. I made an alarm to replace the bleeper supplied with the AIS which had failed. It was made out of an old computer fan, wiring it in to the alarm wires so that when the blades span a thin cable tie made a buzzing noise to warn me of any ships near!

Fish came on board when I wanted them, so my diet was quite varied. I could have meat in the shape of blocks of cured ham that I had bought in Portugal, but apart from that and the fish I was pretty much a vegetarian. Once the fresh bread was used up I started baking my own, and I surprised myself at how good the final product was.

The first six days gave us good progress in excess of 100 miles per day, but then the wind died. I took in all sail and went for a swim - it was strange to see Sarah, my world from outside the boat. Although there was no wind, the swells were still rolling and at about 2 metres high, so at times I was looking down on her, and she looked so very small, vulnerable and insignificant. I was glad to climb back on board. The wind came back, but only gently. We kept moving, and playing around with the self-steering resulted in a setup that kept us vaguely on course, even when the speed dropped down to 2 knots.

Our next problem was weed - the Saragossa kind of stuff that I have seen in the horse latitudes. It kept getting caught in the rudder, and at least once an hour I would have to use the boat hook to clear it. Frequently we had squalls and rain, which was really welcome as I could wash the salt of my skin. I even shaved my head and beard off to make it easier to get rid of the salt crystals. I did not have to waste water washing clothes as I had stopped wearing anything after leaving Mandillo. The solar panel kept up with my electric usage even though it was only 30 watts, and that was even playing music most of the time through my kindle. I only watched a couple of movies on my laptop. Strange as it might seem I was not bored - the sea has always been fascinating to me, but my first meeting with the beast should have warned of what was to come.

Chapter 52

It's funny how vivid my memories are of the first time I saw the sea. I must have been somewhere about 3 years old, it was summer and my father was driving my older sister, my mother and me to a beach in Cornwall. It was hot and sunny, my father had an old red panel van that was quite noisy and slow. We crawled up a steep hill and my sister shouted "look, the sea!" And there it was - shimmering vastness that stretched on forever. I was entranced, and when we eventually arrived on the beach, just about my first action was to sneak off and run straight into the salty argent mass. I do remember being upset when a wave swept me away and I felt so helpless. Luckily, a lady called Jacky (I think) grabbed my hair as I was washed past and hauled me ashore. She visited us about a year or so later and gave me a double-barrelled pop gun. I think some kids just have an instinctive affinity for the medium which will dominate their lives, just as Mozart was into music as a little kid. My cousin Michael spent much of his younger years digging holes in their garden with toy excavators and went on to drive JCBs for a living. My sister was always singing as a little girl, now she has her own band called "Blue Angel" and she is a fine and well-known singer. My first independent action of having a good go at drowning myself on sight of the sea should have tipped off my poor parents as to what lay in the future!

So maybe this explains why I could watch the ocean all day. I have always found it entrancing; what appears at first glance to be a vast waste of nothing much becomes an unending constantly changing world that some are privileged to share if they look and spend the time getting to know the subject. The DVDs remain unwatched. All the books are unread. In my memory are pictures of flying fish in flight, with Tuna and Doradoes also airborne chasing them, rainbows cast by spray thrown up by my boats bow, while dolphins erupt in their "who can get closest" game. A sailfish, magnificent in its colours of purple blue and yellow for its fins, gliding by, curious as to the strange clumsy creature that stays on the surface. Lots of things like this, humpback whales blasting out of the sea to fall back with a awe inspiring "Whumph" - stuff that happens just in front of you, and there is not time to grab a camera. It just happens, and if you are looking you see it, but you have to look.

There is so much to see, and so much to feel. Is it any wonder that after a couple of weeks of this I began to be part of the environment? I began to fit in, I did not resent the weed that slowed us, I did not miss the lost sleep that rising once an hour or so to check sails, course and for any other vessels, that is the lot of the single hander. I looked forward to the gradual brightening of the sky and dawn, and the stars coming out when dusk arrived at the end of the day. I loved the hot sun on my skin and the cooler airs at night. The rain was welcome as was the spray. I could bake bread and cook interesting meals that were not monotonous, well not to me anyway. I was not bored. No, never bored.

There were often jobs to be done, and anything that has to move needs maintenance in the salty environment. Electrical contacts are prone to corrosion and have to be looked at regularly and cleaned. Anything that should not move must be monitored in case it comes loose. The engine had to be started from time to time, and the batteries were checked twice a day. There was a constant round of cleaning and tiding up. There was plenty to do!

Our speed did go down but still we managed more than 80 miles on even the slowest day. For poor Gloria that was a good days run. I was very happy with Sarah's performance, and she seemed to respond to my good will, steering closer to the desired course. It may be that this was just me getting better at setting the self-steering up, but I prefer to think otherwise.

One small fly in the ointment was when I badly cut my finger. In the rush to fit out for the trip I forgot to get a new first aid kid, and the old one only had some plasters and a few bandages in it. I actually did get as far as waiting in a Ferragudo pharmacy to try and buy one but the shop assistant was involved in one of those interminable conversations with another customer that the Portuguese seem to specialise in, so after 10 minutes or so I became fed up and left. In the time after the boat rolled hard and I put a sharp vegetable knife through my finger while I was trying to chop a lime, I began to regret my impatience. It really needed stitching, but I was worried that if I tried it with ordinary cotton the dye would leak and cause an infection. After five days it was not healing up and starting to look swollen and red. I remembered some advice from a character called "long Tom" A Romany gypsy and horse dealer. He told me if ever he had a horse with a bad wound he would treat it with honey. As it happened I had some very good honey on board, one of the things that is wonderful from the Algarve is the honey, this stuff was dark and very tasty, and maybe from lavender. Anyway, I put it on the wound twice a day. The swelling went down the first day and it started to heal up. After four days I no longer had to keep it wrapped, and it began not trouble me apart from a certain numbness that I put down to nerve damage. I was very impressed. Apparently from what I have since read on the internet, raw honey can act as a natural antibiotic, but make sure you use proper honey - cheap products from a supermarket could well be so artificial that it is more like corn syrup and could cause infections. I would definitely use this technique again.

After 10 days of slow progress the trades came back and we started making three figure mileages again. I could now also pick up Barbados radio - they were throwing out a lot of carols and it was very festive. I passed quite close to Barbados during the penultimate night. For a small island it looked very crowded.

Chapter 53

The last 24 hours of the trip was both sad and exciting. I was so in the rhythm of sailing I did not want to stop, but I was really excited about seeing old friends again. I timed it that I was coming into the anchorage past the moored tugs and barges, with the first of the light, under engine with the sails stowed. The first yacht a came too was an old friend of mine called "Hutch" so I anchored near him - a bit too close actually, so I hauled the gear up again and had another go. This time my CQR bit hard and we stopped with 4 metres of depth. I put down all the 8mm chain (14 metres) and 10 metres of nylon rope, which gave us a ratio of about 6 to 1. It was reasonable considering the anchorage could get crowded. I used two heavy stiff ropes of nylon to take all the wear and attached them to the anchor rope with a becket, which is just a loop of rope that is put around the anchor rope a few times then pulled through itself so it grips the rope and does not slip.

I launched my dinghy, but by that time Sally and Paul O'Regan on a catamaran a little way ahead of us had clocked our arrival and were waving, it was so good to see them again! Once the dinghy was floating, I rowed over to Hutch to reacquaint myself with him and see how he had been since last time I had been there. Also I wanted to find out about checking in. He told me that a new office had set up so I did not have to go into the main town, and he was good enough to change some Euros into E.C. dollars for me. He also warned me to buy a curtesy flag or risk getting fined. While I was talking to him a RIB passed by, it was being steered by Jerry Steward, and Paul O'Regan was also on board too. It was great to see them and shake hands. With my new local knowledge, I went off and did the paper work and then went to the slipway restaurant. I saw the chef Kate there, and waited until Dani (Jerry's wife) arrived for a hug and a catch up. Fitzroy came in and brought his dogs down for me to say hello to. In between all of this I managed to get online using the slipway's Wi-Fi so I could contact Eva.

That was only 5 days ago. Sarah is still anchored here in Tyrell bay, and there are changes since I was last here, but not that many. I am surrounded by good friends some old, some new like Janet Hein and Bruce smith, she is a writer and a brilliant photographer, he is an artist and a boat builder. They are fascinating people to be around. I am still busy catching up with all that has gone on since I was here with Gloria in 2011, and I am going to be here when my good friend Pete Evans arrives on the 16th of January so that we can continue our diving escapades. The best news is that Eva is going to take a couple of weeks out of her busy life and join me here in March! Then in the not too distant future lies a return sail to the U.K. (I have to wait here until late May when the Atlantic gales hopefully stop blowing), I will be sorry to leave here again, but glad to get back to Eva and see my family once more. Meanwhile I will enjoy this unspoilt cruising ground and mingle with these friendly people. Right now it is 06.00 local time, the sun is starting to peek out above the hills, and I am going for my early morning swim. Life is good and filled with love and I would not change it for anything.

Max Liberson

Carriacou.

Tyrell Bay, Carriacou, Christmas 2014

Printed in Great Britain
by Amazon